Acknowledgements

First, I want to give thanks to my Lord and Saviour Jesus Christ for blessing me with health and strength, and the skills and talents needed to complete this publication. Also, I am profoundly grateful to all the persons and sources who have contributed to the completion of this publication. Your contributions, encouragement, patience, and support have been instrumental in bringing this project to life.

To my family and friends, thank you for your unwavering confidence in my abilities. Your words of encouragement and moments of understanding have been my guiding light throughout this journey.

I also want to extend my heartfelt appreciation to everyone who has inspired, motivated, and believed in me. This publication is a testament to the collective strength of your support, and for that, I am truly thankful.

Dedication

This publication is dedicated to my incredible mother, Mrs. Pamela Shaw-Rose; my father, Mr. Robert Shirley; my stepfather, Mr. Fitzroy Rose; my loving siblings Joavid, Kristina and Robert; my cherished maternal family; my dear friends who have stood by me; my awesome biological sons Jaiden and Shamar, and my bonus son who God has been most gracious to bless me with, Jonn.

Thank you for believing in me, for your unwavering support, and for being the foundation upon which I build my dreams. This publication is a testament to the love, faith, and the encouragement you have always given me. I am eternally grateful for all of you.

Table of Contents

	Pages
Section A	
Summary Writing	1
Section B	
Expository Writing	22
1) Business Letter	22
2) Letter of Complaint	26
3) Letter of Apology	28
4) Job Application Letter	30
5) Letter of Request	32
6) Letter to the Editor	35
7) Simple Report	38
8) Newspaper Report	47
9) Blogs	50
10) Minutes	51
10) Emails	53
11) Memos	55
12) Notices	57
13) Agenda	59
Section C	
Narrative Writing (The Short Story)	63
Section D	
Argumentative Essay	77
Appendices	82

SECTION A: SUMMARY WRITING

The word limit for this section is 120 words.

A summary is a shortened version of an original piece. It should be in one's own words as much as possible but should mean the same as the original.

Important terms:

    (I)   **Main Idea**
    (II)   **Supporting Details**
    (III) **Paraphrase**

Main Idea

- The main idea of a passage is the central thought or message. It provides a brief overview of the text's main theme or objective. One should think about the important points of the text and the message the author wants to get across to the reader in order to determine the main idea. **A SUMMARY MUST START WITH THE MAIN IDEA, AND THE MAIN IDEA SHOULD BE WRITTEN IN THE ONE'S OWN WORDS.**

- The statement, which expresses the main idea in a paragraph, is called the topic sentence. Often, the topic sentence is the very first sentence in the paragraph. However, it may be anywhere in the paragraph. Usually, the writer states the main idea, then develops or supports the topic sentence with an array of subsidiary or supporting details to prove the main idea.

- The main idea can either be stated or implied. When the main idea of a paragraph is stated, it is most often found in the first sentence of the paragraph. However, the main idea may be found in any sentence of the paragraph.

To find the main idea of any paragraph or passage, ask these questions:
1. Who or what is the paragraph about?
2. What message about the 'who' or 'what' is the author trying to convey?

Main Idea Examples

1) Maria loves spending her weekends outdoors. Every Saturday morning, she wakes up early to go hiking in the nearby mountains. After hiking, she often enjoys a picnic lunch by the lake with her friends. On Sundays, Maria usually takes her dog for a walk in the park and relaxes with a good book under a tree. Being in nature makes her feel happy and refreshed.

The main idea of the paragraph is that Maria enjoys spending her weekends outdoors in nature.

2) Tajhoy's family has a tradition of baking cookies every December. They spend an entire day preparing the ingredients, mixing the dough, and baking dozens of cookies in all sorts of shapes and sizes. Once the cookies are ready, Tajhoy and his siblings decorate them with colourful icing and sprinkles. Afterward, they package the cookies in festive boxes to share with their neighbours and friends, spreading holiday cheer.

The main idea of the paragraph is that Tajhoy's family has a holiday tradition of baking and decorating cookies to share with others.

Main Idea Activities

Activity 1

Read the paragraph and then answer the questions that follow.

But it was at night that Doon Town really blossomed. Along the dark alleys leading off the main street, the prostitutes plied their trade. On the main street itself, stalls lit by flambeaux, yellow flames bending before the wind, lined the pavements, selling oysters with pepper sauce, oranges and black-pudding, their smell mingling with that of the corn being roasted in coal-pots and boiled in oil tins. Fat, picture postcard Negresses, wearing Panama hats and fanning the flames with bits of rolled-up newspaper, called out their wares and solicited the passer-by. Around the entrances to the town's two cinemas struggling crowds gathered and from the rum-shop came the incessant, tuneless maunderings of the drunks. Also, the traffic never stopped. Everything seemed to conspire to produce the illusion of frenzy.

From "FIREFLIES" by Shiva Naipaul

1. What is the main idea of the paragraph?
2. In which sentence is the main idea located?

Activity 2

Directions: Read each passage and write the main idea in the summary box. Remember the main idea must be in one sentence, and it must be in your own words. Afterwards, write an appropriate title for each passage on the lines provided.

1) Clowning isn't always enjoyable. Every time a rodeo clown performs, they put themselves in grave danger. Rodeo clowns jump in front of bulls and make frantic motions to attract their attention when cowboys dismount or when bulls buck them off. Rodeo clowns safeguard the rider by offering a different target in this way. It goes without saying that doing this is extremely risky. You see, clowning around may be serious business at times.

An appropriate title: _____

2) Wolverines are mammals of medium size. The maximum weight they have is fifty pounds. However, by slaying prey that is many times their size, they have gained a reputation for being fierce. But why are they fighting so much? Due to their favoured hunting technique, wolverines likely have a lot of confrontations with other creatures, such as wolves, cougars, and possibly bears. Like other predators, wolverines prefer to eat straight from other hunters rather than pursuing or deceiving their prey. So, a hungry wolverine would try to steal his food while a polar bear or a lone wolf might be feasting on a hard-earned carcass. As you may expect, the wolverine gets into a lot of conflicts because of this hunting method.

An appropriate title: _____

3) Dr. James Naismith was teaching gym at the YMCA College in Springfield, Massachusetts, in December 1891. Dr. Naismith was attempting to keep his students busy despite the rainy weather. He wanted them to engage in a physically demanding game that would keep them on the move. He rejected some of the concepts has they were too harsh. Naismith's breakthrough came next. He drew up the rules for a game in which peach baskets were attached to elevated tracks 10 feet high. Students of Naismith competed with one another by passing the ball and attempting to shoot it into the peach baskets The original game did not feature dribbling. It also took some time to discover that removing the basket bottoms would improve the game's flow. This sport became one of the most well-liked ones in America today. Which game do you think it is?

An appropriate title: _____

4) Where is that buzzing noise coming from? Could it be from the only bird that can fly backwards, the hummingbird? The varied distinctive flight patterns of hummingbirds set them apart from other birds. The hummingbird uses a figure-eight pattern to swing its wings quickly forward and backward, while most other birds flap their wings up and down to fly. As a result, the hummingbird may stay in position. They are also capable of flying upside down and moving quickly. To start flying, other birds have to push off with their feet and gradually increase their speed. The hummingbird may instantly cease flying as well as begin flying at its fastest pace. You won't likely confuse a hummingbird for another bird after having observed one in flight.

An appropriate title: _____

5) Keep in mind that anything worth doing, is worth doing right. With that in mind, the secret to creating flawless cookies is simply preparation and accuracy. First, before baking, make sure you have read the cookie recipe carefully. Before continuing, make sure you have all the ingredients you'll need. Next, make use of quality utensils and tools. A craftsman is sometimes only as good as the tools he uses. Using high-quality instruments reduces errors and enhances the calibre of your output. Finally, use ingredients of the highest calibre. Lead cannot be turned into gold, unlike fairy tale creatures. Using subpar materials will result in subpar products. Therefore, you should utilize the best ingredients available to make great cookies.

An appropriate title: _____

6) Contrary to popular belief, car fuels are not all the same. Diesel, biodiesel, and gasoline are the three fuels that cars may run on. The engine burns all of these fuels to provide the heat and energy needed to move the vehicle. However, these fuels differ significantly from one another. Biodiesel is less common than gasoline and diesel. However, each burn in a unique way. Diesel fuel needs to be compressed before burning since it is heavier and less combustible than gasoline. Despite being lighter than diesel, gasoline is still derived from

crude oil. However, vegetables are used to make biodiesel fuel. Diesel engines, which only run on diesel fuel, must burn both biodiesel and diesel fuel. It is necessary to pump gasoline out of a diesel engine if it is pumped in. Although these fuels may appear to be comparable at the gas station, keep in mind that they differ significantly.

An appropriate title: _____

Activity 3

Each paragraph is followed by four statements. Select the statement that best expresses the main idea. Circle the letter of that statement.

1. Taxes are frequently referred to as being excessively high. In actuality, they are most likely considerably larger than you may have imagined. This is because, in addition to the federal income tax that we are now studying, there are numerous other federal, state, and local taxes such as real estate taxes, sales taxes, inheritance taxes, and state income taxes. These are but a few of the most evident.

      a. Taxes are very high.
      b. We may not be aware of how much we pay in taxes.
      c. Real estate taxes and inheritance taxes are unjust.
      d. Certain taxes are concealed.

2. The public currently views data processing as a mysterious, complex science and considers electronic computers to be enormous brains because of the widespread use of these machines. These two notions are untrue. In essence, a computer is merely a fast-adding device that does tasks as instructed. The computer cannot function if the input data is altered in any way until it is configured to accommodate the changes. Only the incredibly high speed of manipulation makes the business operations it conducts impressive, but the majority of these processes have been in use for decades. The computer, in contrast to humans, can do repetitive calculations without growing bored or weary.

      a. A computer is a mysterious enormous brain.
      b. The speed of a computer makes it impressive.
      c. In many aspects, a computer is better than a human.
      d. A computer is a very fast addition device.

3. The Louisiana Purchase turned out to be one of the most astute economic deals in American history. The country's area doubled as a result of the purchase, which also gave territory from which fourteen new states were partially or entirely formed. Additionally, it allowed for international trade, and granted the United States authority over the mouth of the Mississippi River. The Spanish had shut the river before the acquisition, most likely with Napoleon's consent. Timber, minerals, and a variety of other natural resources were abundant on the purchased land area. The $15 million total cost of the deal was incredibly low: roughly four cents per acre.

    a. The Louisiana Purchase acquired mineral-rich country.
    b. The Louisiana Purchase secured extremely inexpensive land.
    c. The majority of Americans expressed great satisfaction with the purchase.
    d. The United States struck a great business-related deal with the Louisiana Purchase.

4. Many people think that although dogs are man's best friends, coyotes are his worst enemies. Given his love of tiny animals, the coyote has a negative image. He hunts at night and is especially harmful to sheep, young piglets, and chickens. However sometimes it's a good idea to support coyotes. The coyote will frequently clear the land of other animals, such as rabbits, which can destroy crops and some trees, as long as valuable farm animals are safeguarded. He is very helpful in reducing the number of rodents. Ranchers and fruit farmers have found coyotes so beneficial that they would not shoot them any more than they would their dogs in areas where they are allowed to roam freely.

    a. Under certain conditions the coyote is helpful to man.
    b. The coyote is feared because of his fondness for small animals
    c. Modern ranchers would no sooner shoot coyotes than they would shoot dogs.
    d. The coyote usually prefers rabbits and other rodents to sheep and poultry.

5. In the past, anyone with international business that they felt needed to be discussed in person would board a ship and go across the island. Once they were on board, they conducted official business or dealt with social and commercial issues. Aircrafts fly overhead, and ships and people still travel the seven seas today. Yet, words fly through the air above them all. People who are separated by thousands of kilometres can rapidly connect in the most personal way through phone conversations.

    a. Today's overseas phone service eliminates the necessity for any international travel.
    b. In order to resolve issues in business, society, and government, nothing can replace face-to-face communication.
    c. Many of the conversations that used to necessitate going abroad can now be carried out over the phone.
    d. Despite the availability of modern international telephone services, people still take planes or ships to travel overseas.

6. Americans' opinions on gambling are remarkably varied. For instance, you might discover that while horse racing is permitted in a state, one is not allowed to play poker for cash on his front porch. Also, gamblers may face state legal action, but they are still required to obtain a federal license. One church may oppose gambling, while another raises funds by supporting bingo games. It is incredibly difficult to enforce gambling rules because they vary from state to state or even from town to town.
    a. Gambling is viewed negatively by all Americans.
    b. It is challenging to enforce gambling regulations across the USA.
    c. Gambling laws across the USA are very inconsistent, making it a challenge to enforce them.
    d. The opinions of churches regarding gambling are not all the same.

Supporting Details

These are facts or information that contribute to the explanation, or illustration of a text's core topic. The author's main idea is usually supported by facts, figures, quotes, examples, evidence, and descriptions provided in the text. In order to deepen and reinforce the argument or story and help the reader grasp and believe the primary concept more fully, supporting elements are essential. Basically, if you give an idea, you must support it with additional information. Hence, they are called supporting details.

Please see examples below. The supporting details are in ***bold and italics.***

Paragraph 1
My English teacher is awesome. ***She makes learning fun and engaging. She uses creative activities like storytelling and role-playing to help us understand complex literature in a way that's enjoyable. She also takes the time to give each student personalized feedback on our essays, helping us improve our writing skills with specific advice. Additionally, she is always available after class to answer questions and offer extra help, showing that she genuinely cares about our success. Her enthusiasm for the subject is contagious, inspiring all of us to become better readers and writers.***

Paragraph 2
St. James High School is the best school in the parish of St. James. ***The school consistently achieves top rankings in CSEC examinations, with students excelling across various subjects. This reflects its strong emphasis on academic excellence. The teaching staff at St. James High School is composed of highly qualified and experienced teachers who are dedicated to the success of each student, offering personalized attention and support. The school also provides a wide range of extracurricular activities, such as sports, music, drama, and debate clubs, allowing students to develop their talents and interests beyond the classroom. Moreover, St.***

James High School is deeply involved in the local community, encouraging students to participate in community service projects and fostering a strong sense of social responsibility. With a safe and supportive environment and modern facilities like state-of-the-art science labs, a well-stocked library, and excellent sports amenities, St. James High School offers an exceptional educational experience that prepares students for future success.

Activities: Supporting Details

Activity 1
For each main idea below, write a paragraph providing four (4) or more supporting details.
1) Learning a second language offers many benefits to individuals.
2) Exercise is essential for maintaining good physical and mental health.
3) Physical Education should be mandatory in all Jamaican high schools.
4) Recycling is important for protecting the environment.
5) Reading regularly can improve vocabulary and comprehension skills.
6) Technology has greatly changed the way people communicate.
7) A healthy diet is essential for maintaining overall well-being.
8) Volunteering can have a positive impact on both individuals and society.
9) Traveling to new places broadens one's perspective and understanding of different cultures.
10) Good time management skills are crucial for academic success.

Activity 2
Write a paragraph which starts with the main idea below. Give as many details as possible to support the main idea.
Main Idea: Jamaica's rich cultural heritage makes it a unique and vibrant tourist destination.

Activity 3
Write a paragraph that starts with the main idea below. Give as many details as possible to support the main idea.
Main Idea: Social media can have both positive and negative effects on students' academic performance.

Paraphrasing

Rewording a phrase or paragraph to convey the same ideas in a different way while preserving the original meaning is known as paraphrasing. It entails modifying the original text's vocabulary and structure without changing the details or the intended meaning. Translating the original text's meaning into your own words is the main objective of paraphrase. It's critical to maintain the original meaning and refrain from adding any further details or interpretations. One should try to substitute synonyms or other expressions for the original words while paraphrasing. However, keep in mind that some words and phrases, particularly those that are specialized or specific, might not have appropriate synonyms and ought to stay that way.

Effective paraphrase requires not only word replacements but also changes to the sentence structure. This could entail altering the ideas' order, splitting long sentences into shorter ones, or merging sentences. A paraphrase and the original text should not be too similar. Make sure you comprehend the source material completely before paraphrasing it. Inaccurate paraphrase that alters meaning might result from a lack of comprehension of the topic.

Paraphrasing Tips

1) **Understand the Original Text**: Read the text carefully to grasp its meaning before you begin paraphrasing. Ensure you fully understand the main ideas and details.
2) **Use Synonyms**: Replace words in the original text with synonyms that convey the same meaning. Be cautious with technical terms that may not have exact replacements.
3) **Change Sentence Structure**: Alter the structure of sentences by breaking them into shorter ones, combining them, or reordering clauses to create a new flow.
4) **Rephrase Key Phrases**: Reword key phrases and concepts using different expressions while maintaining the original meaning.
5) **Check for Accuracy**: After paraphrasing, compare your version with the original to ensure that the meaning is preserved and that your text is sufficiently different.

Paraphrasing Examples

Paragraph 1:

Jonn has always been passionate about music. He spends hours each day practicing the piano and composing his own songs. On weekends, he attends a music class where he learns about different genres and techniques. Jonn dreams of becoming a professional musician and hopes to perform on big stages one day. Music is not just a hobby for him; it is a significant part of his identity and a way for him to express his emotions.

Paraphrased Answer 1:

Jonn has a deep love for music and dedicates a lot of time daily to playing the piano and creating his own compositions. On weekends, he goes to a music class to learn about various styles and methods. His goal is to become a professional musician and perform on large stages in the future. For Jonn, music is more than just a pastime; it's a crucial aspect of who he is and a means of expressing his feelings.

Paragraph 2:

Eating a balanced diet is crucial for maintaining good health. A diet rich in fruits, vegetables, whole grains, and lean proteins provides the necessary nutrients that our bodies need to function effectively. It also helps prevent chronic diseases such as heart disease, diabetes, and obesity. Additionally, staying hydrated by drinking plenty of water is essential for digestion, circulation, and regulating body temperature.

Paraphrased Answer 2:

Having a well-rounded diet is vital for staying healthy. Consuming a variety of fruits, vegetables, whole grains, and lean proteins supplies our bodies with the essential nutrients required for proper functioning. This kind of diet also plays a role in preventing long-term illnesses like heart disease, diabetes, and obesity. Moreover, keeping hydrated by drinking enough water is important for aiding digestion, maintaining good circulation, and controlling body temperature.

Activity 1-Paraphrasing

Read each sentence carefully. Rewrite each sentence in your own words.
Ensure that the meaning remains the same, but the wording and structure are different.
1) The sun set behind the mountains, casting a golden glow across the valley.
2) She studied hard for the exam and was rewarded with a top score.
3) The city is known for its vibrant nightlife and cultural festivals.
4) They decided to travel by train to enjoy the scenic views along the way.
5) The book provides a comprehensive overview of the history of ancient civilizations.
6) The new policy aims to reduce carbon emissions and promote renewable energy sources.
7) The team worked together to complete the project before the deadline.
8) Eating a balanced diet is essential for maintaining good health and well-being.
9) Technology has greatly transformed the way we communicate and access information.
10) The movie received critical acclaim for its compelling storyline and strong performances.
11) He was delighted to receive a scholarship to support his studies at university.
12) The artist's unique style blends traditional techniques with modern influences.
13) During the meeting, they discussed the plans for the upcoming community event.
14) The weather forecast predicts heavy rain and strong winds for the weekend.
    She has a talent for languages and can speak several fluently.
15) The museum's exhibit showcases artifacts from ancient Egypt.
16) Maintaining a positive attitude can help overcome challenges and achieve goals.
17) The company is launching a new product line to meet growing consumer demand.
18) They visited the historical site to learn more about the local heritage and traditions.
19) The teacher encouraged students to participate actively in class discussions.

Activity 2-Paraphrasing

Read the paragraph carefully, and then paraphrase it. Ensure that the meaning remains the same, but the wording and structure are different.

Jamaica

Jamaica is a beautiful island located in the Caribbean Sea. Known for its awesome beaches, lush rainforests, and vibrant culture, it is a popular tourist destination. The island's diverse landscape includes mountains, rivers, and coastal plains. Jamaica's cultural heritage is rich with influences from its indigenous people, African ancestry, and colonial history. Music plays a significant role in Jamaican culture, with reggae being one of the most famous genres that has originated there. Additionally, the island is known for its delicious cuisine, featuring dishes like jerk chicken and ackee and saltfish.

Activity 3-Paraphrasing

Read the paragraph carefully, and then paraphrase it. Ensure that the meaning remains the same, but the wording and structure are different.

TikTok

TikTok is a social media platform that allows users to create and share short videos with a global audience. Launched in 2016, the app quickly gained popularity due to its user-friendly interface and wide range of creative tools. TikTok videos often feature music, dance routines, comedy sketches, and various challenges. The platform's algorithm promotes content based on user engagement, which helps videos go viral. TikTok has become a cultural phenomenon, influencing trends and shaping popular culture across the world. Its ease of use and engaging content have made it especially popular among

Writing Summaries

Features of a Summary:
a) It is shorter than the original.
b) It reflects the gist or the most important points of the message.
c) It retains the essential meaning in the fewest words possible.
d) It uses language different from the original, that is, it expresses the main idea and main points in new words.
e) It can stand on its own. It is coherent and unified.
f) It starts with the main idea. ALWAYS.
g) It is a short compilation of the main idea and supporting details of an original piece.

Summary Writing Techniques/Rules

1. Determine writer's intention
2. Select the main idea and start your summary with it
3. Combine main ideas
4. Omit all examples
5. Delete all statistical data
6. Omit repetition
7. Use concise language
8. Change direct speech to reported speech
9. Avoid figures of speech and other literary devices. Write literally.
10. Avoid numbering and listing
11. Write in one continuous paragraph
12. Stick to the word limit. The CSEC word limit is 120 words
13. Do not add anything new to the information given to you
14. Avoid commenting on the information. Your job is to summarise.
15. Write in your own words as much as possible
16. Write in the past tense

Summary Writing Steps

1. Read the piece in its entirety and determine the writer's main idea and intent.
2. Write down the main idea in your own words.
3. When there are paragraphs, read the piece paragraph by paragraph and jot down the main points in each paragraph
4. Read the piece again and then go through all you have written down to ensure you have the main idea and all the main points
5. Ensure you have no repetition, examples, figures of speech, illustrations or statistical data
6. Combine all you have written paying attention to the rules of summary writing. Ensure you write in your own words as much as possible.
7. Remember a summary MUST start with the main idea

Summarizing Simple sentences

Tips
   a) Look for groups of words that may be replaced with a collective noun.
   b) Delete repeated or redundant ideas.
   c) Rewrite the sentence using the fewest possible words that mean the same as the original.
   d) Write using your own words as much as possible.

For example:
Original Sentence: Last week Friday, Judith Brown took her daughter who is seven years old to visit the doctor who specializes in children's health and taking care of children.
Answer: Last Friday Judith Brown took her daughter to the paediatrician.

Activity- Summarizing Simple Sentences

Activity 1- Summarize each sentence below in as few words as possible.

1) The accident involving the car, bus, bike, and truck could have been avoided if the driver was not going 250 kilometres per hour in a 50 kilometre per hour zone.
2) In order to maintain a healthy lifestyle, one must ensure that he/she eats all required food from all the food groups on a daily basis.
3) Europe, Asia, North America, South America, Africa, and Antarctica have some of the most beautiful places in the world.
4) It was very unfair for my cousins, uncles, aunts, grandmothers, grandfathers and all my in-laws to turn up at my birthday party without telling anyone they planned to be there.
5) Symonette Hibbert travels to the marketplace in the area where she lives every Saturday at 9am. in order to buy apples, oranges, tomatoes, plums, cabbages, lettuce, pak choi and turnips for the people who live in her household.
6) One of the most commonly practised activities in modern day societies is traveling between two countries on a huge iron mechanical device which has two wings, a tail and four engines, for no other purpose than pleasure.
7) Coffee, made from adding water to grounded cocoa, which is dark brown in colour, is rapidly becoming the preferred drink of many people all over the world.
8) You must know that the reason why my mom, dad, brother, and sister did not come on Tuesday was because the flight that was scheduled to take off at 9pm was put off until the following day at 9 a.m.
9) Man's greatest fear involves not achieving what he set out to do and leaving this world without accomplishing the same.
10) You need to get me pencils, pens, rubbers, rulers, and markers for school.

Activity 2-Contract the following sentences by replacing phrases/clauses with one or two words.

1. Eva Gayle enjoyed the fact that she could speak two languages.
2. Nicky Chin worked at a place where the children had no parents.
3. She was involved in an accident that resulted in her death.
4. The people in the church listened keenly to the pastor Sandra Thomas' sermon.
5. People who drive are often encouraged to be considerate of people who are walking.

6. Last night, Maureen James read a story that had a writer whose name was not given.
7. That tribe is filled with people who eat humans.
8. In the event that Nadia Robinson does not return, please start the meeting without her.
9. The football match ended without any team winning the game.
10. I found Kemoya Williams' handwriting to be quite difficult to read.

Activity 3- Summarize each sentence.

1) Increases in the movement of the population, food and livestock, added to an increase in the use of fossil fuels, pollution from cars and factories and other pollution from industrial chemicals are all destroying the earth.
2) University professors who have often worked in the same institutions for years and years are experts in their fields of interest and study and have more than likely written numerous books.
3) Swine flu, a strain of the H1N1 influenza virus is a strange and harmful viral infection which is currently sweeping across the globe, instigating both sickness and death and causing people to fall in states of pandemonium and chaos.
4) Last summer on my trip to the Holy Land of Jerusalem, I visited the Christian place of worship, the Jewish place of worship and the Muslim place of worship over a 7-day period.
5) The moment I saw Jessica Richards, my father's mother, I knew something was wrong. She was about one hundred and ten pounds and not her usual 250 pounds.

Passages to Summarise

Example of an Original Passage and the Passage's Summary

Passage

Somewhere in the archives of our radio stations and in a few private collections are recordings of the song entitled "Trees". It would have been composed and recorded years ago when the world was not as conscious as it is now about our environment. However, it was the majesty and sturdiness of trees that moved the lyricist, in accepting their importance, to observe that, whatever might be our many achievements and creations on the planet, "only God can make a tree".

The importance of trees as part of our environment is often undermined as millions of acres of land all over the world are cleared of trees and more land is put into agriculture or the trees are replaced by concrete buildings, signifying one concept of economic development.

At the same time, those who are aware of the importance of having trees around are heard warning that we need to display a sense of balance. For while we, as inhabitants of the planet, need land for food and for erecting houses and so on, the planet itself requires trees if it is to adequately sustain life. These life forms include us. With all this in mind, it has been most heartening to learn that steps are being taken in our part of the woods to plant at least 80 000 more trees, one for every person below the age of 18.

According to one environmental expert, "When people build, they tend to just clear the land rather than build around existing vegetation. Then they plant a small flower garden." He stressed that these could not replace the diminished oxygen production caused by the removal of trees, or the role played by trees in conserving our mainly shallow soil. When we see muddy water rushing by after rainfall, it is the result of soil being washed away from areas that have no tree roots to hold it in place.

A consciousness of how we should act as stewards of the planet does not just happen. We have to be carefully taught. This tree-planting project is an example of how we can teach our young people what is expected of them and what is required in the years ahead if we are not to disadvantage later generations.

Summary (Answer)

Trees are extremely essential for sustaining life on earth, but deforestation for agriculture and construction disrupts the environment. While development is necessary, trees play a crucial role in producing oxygen and preventing soil erosion. Small gardens cannot replace the important role that trees play; hence it is unwise to destroy trees. To maintain a healthy balance, it is important to preserve trees and educate younger generations about their significance. Planting trees helps foster a sense of responsibility and stewardship, ensuring that future generations understand the need to protect natural resources. By recognizing the importance of trees, we can work toward a sustainable future and act as responsible caretakers of the planet.

Past CXC Passages to Summarise

Practice Passage 1

Summarise in 120 words or fewer

Coconut Oil Redeemed

For several decades, Caribbean people have used coconut oil, a local product, for different purposes including hair dressing and cooking. The oil was refined and turned into cooking oil. Some Caribbean islands, including Trinidad and Tobago, exported the oil to foreign markets.

The 1980s saw the downfall of coconut oil. Studies conducted among people who suffered heart attacks linked cholesterol found in coconut oil with the disease. They claimed that the saturated fats were responsible for the condition. Nutritionists bypassed coconut oil in favour of corn oil and other vegetable oils.

Local edible oil manufacturers were not convinced. They protested that the goal of manufacturers of corn oil was to get a bigger share of the international market for their product. Their protests were not taken seriously. The scientific evidence provided by these international groups gained the attention of consumers. As a result of the research, health-conscious communities favoured corn oil and other vegetable oil like soybean and sunflower oil over coconut oil.

After years of testing, there is no conclusive evidence that a higher intake of cholesterol will inevitably increase the incidence of heart attacks. Furthermore, the more recent scientific evidence available has shown that the previous negative labels attached to coconut oil are unfounded. Research conducted on the matter by the Tropical Metabolism Research Unit at the University of the West Indies indicates that by itself no risk of heart disease arises from the use of coconut

In the Philippines, the positive findings with respect to coconut oil are of significant value. In that country, coconut oil forms a high part of the normal dietary intake, averaging six percent of calories consumed. However, the rate of cardiovascular disease is much lower than that in the US where the intake of coconut oil is negligible. Further, there is no connection in the Philippines or the US between coconut oil consumption and heart disease.

A return to the normal consumption of coconut oil, instead of the imported products, could revitalize a traditional, rural-based, labour-intensive industry and provide a boost to the economies of the Caribbean. It is a locally produced fat and its reacceptance in the daily dietary regimen of the population could stimulate areas of agriculture which have been sorely neglected during the last decade.

Adapted from the Editorial, Trinidad Guardian, 16 March, 1992, p. 8.

Practice Passage 2: Putting Children to Sleep

Make a summary, describing the ways to solve the problems of putting young children to bed. Your account should not be more than 70 words.

A growing child still requires a decent amount of sleep, and for young schoolchildren and toddlers, that's between 10 and 12 hours a night.
But what happens when children fight it every step of the way, from taking a bath to putting on pyjamas to getting into bed? When they refuse to sleep alone in bed or wake up repeatedly, or need to be rocked for an hour before nodding off?
It's usually not hard to tell when a child doesn't get enough sleep.
"He can be irritable, whiny, clumsier," says paediatrician Dr Leigh Shapleigh. "And when a child has any sort of behaviour problem, it is just exacerbated by lack of sleep."

Children - especially small children - thrive on routine, so the more regular their bedtime is the better it is for the entire family.

Exactly when a child goes to bed has to be determined by the parents, Shapleigh says.

"The trick is to decide what you want to do. If you want the bedtime at 7.30 or 8.30 or 9.30, decide how to get there."

Although many parents are consistent, the routine they adopt only results in long, wearying nights. They become caught in a trap they have inadvertently created. Their children rely on them to help get to sleep. Parents cajole, sing to them, rock them, rub their back -- only to have the little ones wake the moment they tiptoe out of the room. Quality time disappears, tempers are short, and bedtime becomes a civil war.

To frazzled parents who want desperately to escape that trap, Shapleigh suggests the method that worked for a number of families.

"You have to let them cry. Be there to reassure them. Leave a night light on but be consistent. They understand your behaviour more than they do your words."

Dr Richard Ferber, a paediatrician who is sometimes called the Dr Spock of children's sleep problems, assures parents that most bedtime conflicts are not serious, and they can be avoided.

Parents who choose to wait out their child's erratic sleep patterns will probably see them disappear, but that could take months or years.

Instead of waiting, Ferber suggests that parents take action, and after following a pleasant bedtime routine, put the children to bed, leaving them there even if they cry, but checking on them at specific intervals.

"There is no way to treat this problem without listening to some crying, but you can keep it to a minimum," he says.

Parents who are fighting the sleep battle with their children often complain of being tired, but forget that their children, who haven't yet learned to complain, are also tired.

"It is in your child's best interests to have uninterrupted sleep," Ferber says.

For children as well as adults, Ferber says, "sleep (serves) some restorative function for our bodies and perhaps for our minds, and it is certainly necessary for normal functioning during the day."

Practice Passage 3

Summarize in your own words, the advantages and disadvantages of owning a television. Your account should not be more than 90 words.

With the invention of televisions, many forms of entertainment have been replaced. Lively programs like television serials and world news have removed from us the need to read books or papers, to listen to radios or even to watch movies. In fact, during the 1970s, when televisions were first introduced, cinema theatres suffered great losses as many people chose to stay in the comforts of their homes to watch their favourite programs.

Indeed, the television brings the world into our house. Hence, by staying at home and pressing some buttons world happenings are immediately presented before us. Children nowadays develop faster in language, owing to their early exposure to television programs. At such a tender age, it would be difficult for them to read books or papers. Thus, television programs are a good source of learning for them. Furthermore, pronunciations by the newscasters, actors or actresses are usually standardized, hence young children watching these programs will learn the 'right' pronunciations too. Owning a television is also extremely beneficial to working parents who are usually too busy or tired to take their kids out for entertainment. Surrounded by the comforts of their home, the family can have a chance to get together and watch their favourite television programs.

Of course, we should not be too carried away by the advantages of television and overlook its negative points. Watching television programs takes away our need to read. Why bother to read the papers when we can hear them from the television news reports? Why read books when exciting movies are screened? The lack of reading is unhealthy especially to younger children as they will grow up only with the ability to speak but not write. I have a neighbour whose six-year-old child can say complete sentences like "I like cats," but when told to write out the sentence, is unable to do so. Not only are the writing skills of children affected, but their thinking capacities are also handicapped. Television programs remove the need to think. The stories, ideas and facts are woven in the way television planners wanted. Exposure to such opinions and the lack of thinking opportunities will hinder the children's analysing ability.

Despite the disadvantages of watching television programs, personally, I think that choosing the 'middle path', which is to do selective television viewing and not overindulging in the habit should be the best solution to reconcile both the merits and demerits of owning a television.

Practice Passage 4

Summarize in not more than 90 words, the advantages and disadvantages of advertisements.

We are bombarded by many advertisements every day. Vendors try all means and ways to gain our attention and sell us their products or services. Advertisements appear everywhere, on television programs, radios, in the papers, magazines, pamphlets and so on. Advertisements are actually very useful though we sometimes feel annoyed when they interrupt our favourite television programs. They provide us with free information on the products and services. There are two types of advertisements. The informative advertisements are the ones which provide us with the details of the products or services. This information is especially useful if the product or service is new. For instance, when we need to buy a computer, advertisements describing the latest models, and their different functions would be extremely helpful. However, only a minority of the advertisements are informative ones. Many of them belong to the second category, the persuasive kind. These advertisements not only tell us more about the products, at the same time, they persuade customers to buy them by claiming that their products are superior to the rivalry ones. These claims may sometimes be untrue.

Besides being informative and persuasive, advertisements also help to subsidize the prices of magazines and newspapers. Our newspapers are sold at a low price of about one dollar, owing to the advertisements in the papers; otherwise, the price would have been higher.

While advertisements can be good helpers for shopping, they do have their shortcomings. Most advertisements aim to sell only. Faults of the products or services are usually hidden from the consumers. Hence, sometimes, we feel deceived if the product or service we bought does not turn out the way the advertisements claim to be. Sometimes, advertisements by rival competitors can get very intensive, especially when there are many firms producing similar products. One common example is washing powder. There are so many advertisements for the different brands that customers sometimes get confused over what they should buy. Furthermore, having more advertisements would mean that the production cost of the firm would be increased. These rises in cost are usually passed on to the consumers in the form of higher prices.

Hence, in conclusion, though I do advocate advertisements, I do not deny their flaws. Without them, we might have to buy things based on incomplete information or go through more complicated ways before getting to know the products or services. On the other hand, too many advertisements also complicate our buying decisions. So, I would say that we cannot live without advertisements, but we must be careful how we live with them.

Practice Passage 5

Make a summary of not more than 100 words, describing the various means of transportation.

The means of transportation have changed and improved over many centuries. Long ago, during the times of the kings and knights, animals such as horses, buffaloes and camels were used by man for transportation purposes. These animals no doubt did save man from traveling by foot, they took a long time to complete the journeys, especially when transporting goods.

In 1825, George Stephenson's opening of the first railway marked significant progress in the history of transportation. Railways were in popular demand because they could carry more people and loads. More importantly, they ran faster than animals. Railways improved communication networks and hence, imports and exports of goods and people traveling out of their towns or even countries to work were made possible. Unfortunately, since the invention of motor vehicles, the popularity of railways has declined.

Motor vehicles were first invented in the eighteenth century. These vehicles were preferred by many people as they do not run on tracks and hence do not have fixed routes. Travelers can then plan their own routes to suit their convenience. This is especially so when the destinations are places like small towns or remote areas. In these places, few or even none of the trains ever reach them; so, traveling by motor vehicle would solve this problem. Over many years of modifications, the motor vehicle is now one of the most used means of transportation. Today, we travel in cars, taxis, buses, lorries or vans almost every day.

Another form of transportation is by water. It may be the slowest but the cheapest form of bulk transportation. Though over the centuries of innovations, water transportation has improved from the ancient wind dependent yachts to the modern motor driven ships, journeys by water are still characterized by the dangers and unpredictability of meeting natural disasters like the storms.

The evolution of world transportation has reached its pinnacle with the invention of airplanes. Transportation by plane is the easiest and fastest. Planes gliding smoothly in the air are not obstructed by seas, hills, buildings and so on. Though convenient, this means of transport is the most expensive. Despite the popular demand, the transportation network of the planes is still not a balanced and complete one till today. Developed countries tend to make use of air transportation more frequently than the less developed ones as they do more exporting and importing of goods and have more people traveling to and from their countries. Hence, the networks in these developed countries are denser.

Practice Passage 6

Summarize the passage below in not more than 80 words

Communication is part of our everyday life. We greet one another, smile or frown, depending on our moods. Animals too, communicate, much to our surprise. Just like us, interaction among animals can be both verbal and non-verbal.

Singing is one way in which animals can interact with one another. Male blackbirds often use their melodious songs to catch the attention of the females. These songs are usually rich in notes variation, encoding various kinds of messages. Songs are also used to warn and keep off other blackbirds from their territory, usually a place where they dwell and reproduce.

Large mammals in the oceans sing too, according to adventurous sailors. Enormous whales groan and grunt while smaller dolphins and porpoises produce pings, whistles and clicks. These sounds are surprisingly received by other mates as far as several hundred kilometres away.

Besides singing, body language also forms a large part of animals' communication tactics. Dominant hyenas exhibit their power by raising the fur hackles on their necks and shoulders, while the submissive ones normally "surrender" to the powerful parties by crouching their heads low and curling their lips a little, revealing their teeth in friendly smiles.

Colours, which are most conspicuously found on animals, are also important means of interaction among animals. Male birds of paradise, which have the gaudiest coloured feathers often hang themselves upside down from branches, among fluffing plumes, displaying proudly their feathers, attracting the opposite sex.

The alternating black and white striped coats of zebras have their roles to play too. Each zebra is born with a unique set of stripes which enables its mates to recognize them. When grazing safely, their stripes are all lined up neatly so that none of them loses track of their friends. However, when danger such as a hungry lion approaches, the zebras would dart out in various directions, making it difficult for the lion to choose his target.

Insects such as the wasps, armed with poisonous bites or stings, normally have brightly painted bodies to remind other predators of their power. Hoverflies and other harmless insects also make use of this fact and coloured their bodies brightly in attempts to fool their predators into thinking that they are as dangerous and harmful as the wasps too.

SECTION B: EXPOSITORY WRITING

Excluding memos and notices, the word limit for this section is 200-250 words.

Writing with the intention of explaining or informing in an understandable and direct way is known as expository writing. Expository writing's primary goal is to give readers accurate information and insightful analysis on a certain topic by utilizing examples, logical arguments, and supporting data. This type of writing is frequently seen in reports, manuals, letters, textbooks, essays, and articles.

Key Features of Expository Writing:

1) **Clear and Concise Language**: Avoid using unclear or overly complex terminologies in your writing; instead, keep it simple and easy to read.
2) **Logical Organization**: To make it easier for the reader to follow the writer's line of reasoning, information is usually arranged logically. When this step-by-step process is given, the information can be easily followed.
3) **Objective Tone:** Factual and objective writing makes up expository writing. The author doesn't share any personal thoughts or feelings when presenting the material.
4) **Use of Evidence:** The information presented provides credibility and is supported by facts, figures, examples, and quotes.
5) **Clearly Stated Thesis**: The thesis or central idea is expressed in concise terms.

The Business Letter

A business letter is an official letter that is sent between businesses or between the company and its customers, clients, or other external parties. Generally speaking, business letters are intended to request things, reply to questions, provide updates, and uphold professional connections. Business letters adhere to a particular format and tone in contrast to informal or personal letters in order to guarantee efficiency, professionalism, and clarity.

Characteristics of a Business Letter

1) **Formal Tone:** A business letter should not contain any slang or colloquial language. Instead, it should be written in a courteous, professional manner. **DO NOT WRITE WITH CONTRACTIONS, for example, "you'll" and "don't."**
2) **Clear Purpose:** The letter should make sure the recipient knows why it is being sent right away by outlining it in the first paragraph.
3) **Structured Format:** Business letters usually have a predetermined format. It should also be in paragraph form. All paragraphs must be indented. **WHEN WRITING, DO NOT SKIP A LINE FOR A NEW PARAGRAPH. INSTEAD, GO IN A NEW LINE AND INDENT.**
4) **Conciseness:** Business letters are brief and direct, omitting unnecessary information and concentrating on the core idea.

5) **Particular Content:** The information should be pertinent and particular to the subject matter, frequently containing specifics like dates, sums, and any steps that the recipient must take.
6) **Professional Closing:** The letter is concluded with a formal phrase like "Sincerely," "Your respectfully," or "Yours faithfully," and is signed and printed with the sender's name. Only the first letter of the first word in the closing is capitalised. For example, "Yours truly."

Parts of a Business Letter

1. Heading (This contains the Sender's Address and Date)
- **Sender's Address**: This includes the address of the person writing the letter. If the letter is written on company letterhead, the sender's address is usually already included at the top of the page.
- **Date**: The date should be placed one line below the sender's address. It indicates when the letter was written.

2. Inside Address
- This is the address of the recipient. Include the recipient's name, title, company, and full address. If you don't know the specific person's name, you may address the letter to a department.

3. Salutation
- The salutation is the greeting in the letter. Use a formal greeting, such as "Dear," followed by the recipient's title and last name. If you don't know the recipient's name, use a general salutation such as "Dear Sir or Madam."

4. Subject Line
- The subject line indicates the main topic or purpose of the letter. It helps the reader quickly understand the reason for the communication.

5. Body
- The body of the letter is where you write the main content. It should be clear, concise, and logically structured, typically divided into paragraphs.

6. Closing
- The closing is a polite way to end the letter. Use a formal closing phrase, followed by a comma. Common closings include "Sincerely," "Yours truly," or "Yours faithfully."

7. Signature
- The signature section includes the signature of the sender followed by the sender's name and position (if necessary). If it's an email or digital letter, the typed name alone may suffice. Some people use a digital signature.

Business Letter Format

The block and semi-block formats are the two main formats used for the business letter.

1) The block and semi-block letter formats are distinguished by their uncomplicated and well-structured look. All letter components in a block letter format are aligned to the left margin. Paragraph indents are not used in typing, only in writing. **THE BLOCK FORMAT IS THE MOST COMMONLY USED BUSINESS LETTER FORMAT.**
2) Similar to the block format, the semi-block style aligns most of the letter's components to the left margin. However, paragraphs are indented (both when writing and while typing), and elements like the sender's address, date, closing, and signature are positioned to the right. The closing, and signature, are usually right aligned to match the sender's address and the date. If a company uses a letterhead, only the date, closing, and signature, are right aligned.

NB: WHEN HANDWRITING (FOR BOTH FORMATS), YOU SHOULD ALWAYS SKIP A LINE AFTER EACH SECTION, EXCEPT WHEN MOVING TO A NEW PARAGRAPH. WHEN MOVING INTO A NEW PARAGRAPH, GO INTO A NEW LINE AND INDENT.

Block-Format Example

ABC Company
1234 Market Street
Montego Bay
St. James
(876) 123-4567
abc@abccompany.com

July 26, 2024

Mrs. Tashoy Harper-Brooks
The Sales and Purchasing Manager
XYZ Corporation
5678 Industrial Lane
Falmouth
Trelawny

Dear Mrs. Harper-Brooks,

RE: Proposal for Supply Chain Partnership

    I am writing to suggest that ABC Company and XYZ Corporation collaborate strategically in the supply chain. Being a top provider of superior raw materials, we are in a unique position to accommodate your production facilities' expanding requirements.

    A few major advantages of our collaboration would be reduced costs, improved inventory control, and expedited shipping. We have effectively worked with a number of elite manufacturers, and we are sure that XYZ Corporation will benefit from our experience and knowledge.

    I appreciate you taking a look at this suggestion. I am excited for the chance to talk about how we can collaborate to succeed as a team. If you need more information or have any questions, please do not hesitate to contact the undersigned at the telephone number or email address listed above.

Sincerely yours,
__M. Webster_____
Marcel Webster
Sales Manager

Semi-Block Format Example

                                                                     ABC Company
                                                                     1234 Market Street
                                                                     Montego Bay
                                                                     St. James
                                                                    (876) 123-4567
                                                                    abc@abccompany.com

                                                                    July 26, 2024

Mr. Ceon Shaw
The Sales and Purchasing Manager
XYZ Corporation
5678 Industrial Lane
Falmouth
Trelawny

Dear Mr. Shaw:
                              RE: Proposal for Supply Chain Partnership

    I am writing to suggest that ABC Company and XYZ Corporation collaborate strategically in the supply chain. Being a top provider of superior raw materials, we are in a unique position to accommodate your production facilities' expanding requirement.

    A few major advantages of our collaboration would be reduced costs, improved inventory control, and expedited shipping. We have effectively worked with a number of elite manufacturers, and we are sure that XYZ Corporation will benefit from our experience and knowledge.

I appreciate you taking a look at this suggestion. I am excited for the chance to talk about how we can collaborate to succeed as a team. If you need more information or have any questions, please do not hesitate to contact the undersigned at the telephone number or email address listed above.

                                                                              Sincerely yours,
                                                                             ___S. Christie_____
                                                                             Shamar Christie
                                                                             Sales Manager

The Letter of Complaint

- To complain means to voice dissatisfaction about someone or something.
- The letter of complaint is a business letter used by a customer to voice dissatisfaction to a company or organization about a product or service. It is usually written in four paragraphs.

Outline

- **Paragraph 1-** Voice the dissatisfaction. Include all necessary dates, times, amount, product names and brands, and any other relevant information.
- **Paragraph 2-** Explain what happened in detail and tell how you were inconvenienced.
- **Paragraph 3-** As is necessary, explain the response of the persons involved.
- **Paragraph 4-** Say what needs to be done to remedy the situation. Include your contact information if it was not included in the heading. Politely close the letter.

<u>Example</u>
Capital Heights
Green Pond
Montego Bay #1 P.O.
St. James

April 29, 2024

Mr. Jerry Shaw
The Manager
ABC Home and Things
Orange Hill
Montego Bay

Dear Mr. Shaw,
<u>RE: Defective Alarm Clock</u>

This is a complaint about a defective alarm clock that I purchased from your organization on April 27, 2024, at about 3: 45 pm. The cost of the clock was three thousand five hundred dollars. ($3500.00). It was a ZTE Alarm Clock.

When I purchased the clock, the salesclerk Jordene Godfrey told me it has two weeks warranty. However, after one day's use it began to malfunction. It does not alarm on time, and it goes off at any random time. Sometimes, it does not alarm at all. This has really inconvenienced me as I am a student who works and studies late, and I need the clock to wake me up for my study periods, and for work.

I took back the clock and my receipt to the store on April 28, 2024. I was told by the cashier that you are out of office. I spoke to the same salesclerk but was rudely told that I cannot get a refund or replacement. She even insinuated that I had destroyed the clock. Disappointed, I eventually went home with the defective clock.

As the manager, I need you to do something about this urgently. I need a refund or a new clock by May 1, 2024. I hope that for a continued great business relationship, this matter will be addressed shortly. For further information, you may contact the undersigned at 876-222-2222 or abc@gmail.com. I await a favourable response.

Sincerely yours,

___J. McBean___
Jaiden McBean

Letter of Complaint Activities

Question 1: Your name is Derrick Shaw. On Saturday, August 10, 2024, you purchased ten pounds of pork, ten pounds of mutton, and twenty pounds of chicken from Johnson's Meat Mart located at 10 Church Lane in Montego Bay, St. James, for a dinner party on Monday, August 12, 2024. You stored the meat in your freezer after purchasing it. However, when you tried to thaw, clean, and season the meat on Sunday, August 11, 2024, you discovered that all of it had spoiled. Since the shop was closed on Sunday, you returned the meat on Monday, August 12, 2024. The manager was unavailable, and the staff was rude when you explained the situation, so you left with the spoiled meat. Write a complaint letter to Mr. Grege Johnson, the manager, explaining what happened and requesting a refund or replacement.

Question 2: Your name is Rasheed McDonald. You bought a blender from King's Home and Things on August 15, 2024. It is located at 11 Shirley Way, Montego Bay, St. James. When you tried to use it the following day, you realized it wasn't working properly. You returned the blender to the store on August 17, 2024, but the manager was not present, and none of the employees helped you. Write a complaint letter to the store manager, Ms. Marlene Shaw, describing the problem and asking for either a replacement or a refund.

Question 3: Your name is Kingsley Shaw. On August 18, 2024, you booked a cleaning service with Superior Services Ltd. It is located at 19 Chance Boulevard in Montego Bay, St. James. The cleaners arrived late and did not complete the work as promised. Areas like the living room and kitchen were left uncleaned, and the staff was unprofessional. After raising your concerns, they dismissed your complaints. Write a letter to the Customer Service Manager, Ms. Ila Gentles, explaining the situation and requesting a refund for the incomplete service.

The Letter of Apology

The following are important in a good business letter of apology

- **Say you're sorry.**
- **Own the mistake.** It's important to show the wronged person that you're willing to take responsibility for your actions.
- **Describe what happened.** The wronged person needs to know that you understand what happened and why it was hurtful to them. Make sure you remain focused on your role rather than deflecting the blame.
- **Have a plan.** Let the wronged person know how you intend to fix the situation.
- **Admit you were wrong.** It takes a big person to own up to being wrong.
- **Ask for forgiveness.** A little vulnerability goes a long way toward proving that you mean what you say.

Outline

Paragraph 1- Apologize and say what you are sorry for
Paragraph 2- Explain what happened, not to deflect blame but so the person may understand. Also mention what your company's goal is for all customers.
Paragraph 3- Say what you will do to make up for your wrong
Paragraph 4- Apologize again, ask for forgiveness and politely close.

Example

ABC Office Equipment
2 Orange Hill
Montego Bay
St. James

March 3, 2024

Ms. Peta-Gaye Jones
874 Granville Avenue
Montego Bay
St. James

Dear Ms. Jones:

<u>RE: Poor Customer Service Experience</u>

On behalf of ABC Office Equipment, we extend our sincerest apologies for the poor experience you had with our sales associate, Ren Stewart. We understand that he made unprofessional remarks when you visited our store to inquire about a new copier on February 28, 2024. You came to us in search of information, and instead were subjected to a rude salesperson.

At ABC, it is our goal to help all customers make an informed purchase decision without having to deal with aggressive sales tactics. Mr. Stewart is a new employee that is in training. We take full responsibility for his behaviour. He has received a written reprimand and will be shadowing one of our senior sales associates until he has a better understanding of the ABC Office Equipment approach to customer service.

We are grateful that you brought this issue to our attention, and we ask your forgiveness. We assure you that this will not happen again. You have been a loyal customer over the years, and we sincerely appreciate your business. To express our sincerest apologies, we have included a voucher for 50 % off your next purchase over $50,000 in our store.

Again, we sincerely apologize, and we hope our great business relationship will continue for many years to come. For further information, please feel free to visit us at the above address, call us at 876-222-2222 or email us at abcoe@outlook.com.

Sincerely yours,
    L. Croll
Lourama Croll
Equipment Sales Manager

Letter of Apology Activities

Question 1: You are the owner of A & E Office Supplies located at 14 Orange Hill, Montego Bay, St. James. Recently, you received a complaint from Ms. Sandrae Vincent, who lives at Lot 6262 in Cornwall Gardens, Westmoreland. She is upset because the order she placed and paid for online on August 10, 2024, which included 14 packs of typing sheets and a printer, has not been delivered. Ms. Vincent was told the items would arrive by August 14, 2024, but she did not receive them. Additionally, none of her calls or emails have been answered, and since she lives far away, she cannot come to the store to pick up the order. Write an apology letter to Ms. Vincent, explaining what happened and offering a solution.

Question 2: You own a restaurant. On August 15, 2024, a customer named Ian Shaw visited to celebrate his birthday. Unfortunately, he was treated poorly by one of the waitresses Albertine George during his visit. Mr. Shaw lives at Lot 1345 Farm Heights, Montego Bay, St. James. Write a letter of apology to Mr. Shaw, acknowledging the incident and assuring him that steps will be taken to ensure it doesn't happen again. Be sure to include the name and address of your restaurant in the letter.

Question 3: You are Franz Clarke, the manager of Tech World, a technology store located at 25 King Street, Kingston. Recently, you received a complaint from a customer, Ms. Angella Shaw, who purchased a laptop on August 5, 2024. Ms. Shaw reside at 19 Meadow Street in Spanish Town, St. Catherine. After using the laptop for just two days, Ms. Shaw encountered multiple issues, including slow performance and frequent crashing. Ms. Shaw returned the laptop on August 10, 2024, but the staff was unhelpful and did not offer her a solution. Write an apology letter to Ms. Shaw, acknowledging the poor customer service and offering a resolution to the problem.

The Job Application Letter

When applying for jobs, you often send or upload a resume or curriculum vitae along with a cover letter, also called a job application letter. In contrast to your resume, which provides a summary of your accomplishments and work history, your job application letter tells the company why you are the best candidate for the job and deserve to be chosen for an interview.

Format of the Body of the Letter

This is usually in three distinct parts or paragraphs.

1) **In the first paragraph,** you'll want to mention the job you are applying for and where you saw the job listing. You will also want to say how your skills and experience qualify you for the position
2) **The next paragraph** is the most important part of your letter. This is where you basically "sell" yourself. You will share the relevant details on your experience, character and accomplishments which make you the best candidate. You should also ensure that you mention your co-curricular or volunteer involvement. This is to show that you are well rounded.
3) **The third and last paragraph** of the body of the letter will be your "thank you" to the employer. You may also offer follow-up information.

Job Application Letter Sample

Lot 010101 Cornwall Courts
Montego Bay #2 P.O.
St. James
876-888-8888/ity@gmail.com

March 4, 2024

Mrs. Tameika Reid-Williams
The Manager
XYZ Loan Financing Company
Shop #5 Overton Plaza
Montego Bay, St. James

Dear Mrs. Reid-Williams,

RE: DATA ENTRY OPERATOR

      With reference to your advertisement in the Western Mirror dated March 1, 2024, I would like to express my interest in an entry-level data entry operator position with XYZ Company. Throughout my job search and conversations with others in the field of loan financing, I have come to respect the professionalism that characterizes your firm and its employees. I am confident that XYZ Company's values and objectives would highly complement my own strengths and enthusiasm.

      I am a recent graduate who would love to use this opportunity to promote the continued growth and development of your company and enhance my personal development. I am dedicated, hardworking, organized and trustworthy and I am known for going the extra mile to ensure tasks are done efficiently and on time. I also find great pleasure and fulfilment in taking part in extracurricular activities.

      Please review the enclosed resume. I am interested in participating in a personal interview. I look forward to hearing from you. Thank you for your consideration.

Yours respectfully,
   K. Chambers-Knock
Kem Chambers-Knock (Mrs.)

Job Application Letter Activities

Question 1: You recently graduated from HEART Trust NTA with a Level 3 Diploma in Early Childhood Education. On August 18, 2024, you were on Caribbeanjobs.com and saw a job opening for an Early Childhood Teacher at Little Scholars Preparatory School, located at 8 Hillcrest Avenue, Kingston 6. You are passionate about working with young children and believe you have the skills and qualifications for the role. Write a job application letter to Ms. Prudence Shaw, the principal, expressing your interest in the position and outlining your relevant training and experience.

Question 2: You are interested in applying for the role of Administrative Assistant at Jamaica Commercial Bank located at 15 King Street, Montego Bay, St. James. You saw the position advertised in The Gleaner on August 10, 2024. With your background in business administration and two years of experience in a similar role, you believe you are the right fit for this position. Write an application letter to Ms. Kersha Reid, the bank's Human Resources Manager, to apply for the role, outlining your qualifications and suitability.

Question 3: On August 12, 2024, a new hotel called Tropical Breeze Resort, located at 22 Sunshine Avenue, Ocho Rios, St. Ann, published a job advertisement in The Jamaica Observer. The hotel is looking to fill multiple vacancies, including positions for chefs, housekeepers, waitstaff, and front desk agents. Write a letter applying for the position of your choice. Address the letter to the Human Resources Manager, Ms. Georgia Matthews explaining why you are the ideal candidate for the job.

Letter of Request

A request letter is a respectful way of asking for certain documents, permission, or information from people or organizations. The purpose of a request letter depends upon the kind of request or favour the individual is asking. It should be in 3-4 paragraphs. How each paragraph is structured is dependent on the type of request.

Letter of Request Sample #1

123 Main Street
Farm Heights
Montego Bay #1 P.O.
St. James
tb@gmail.com/876-777-7777

March 10, 2024

Mrs. Joneisha Dwyer-White
The Students Loan Director
City Bank
222 Main Street
Montego Bay
St. James

Dear Mrs. Dwyer-White,

<u>RE: Application Request for Education Loan</u>

  I would like to request an education loan from Citibank for my postgraduate studies in the United States of America. I have received **a** letter of acceptance for admission from the University of North Carolina.

I need a loan amount of JMD $1,000,000.00 for study purposes. The details of the course and university information are attached to this mail. You may also visit the official university site www.unc.edu.jm for more information.

The postgraduate course is for four semesters or two years. There is a paid internship after the course as mentioned in the details of the university. Later in this program, I will choose a job which will start my personal income and enable me to repay my loan regularly and quickly.

As collateral, I have attached my parents' property documents. Kindly check the requisite documents and confirm your take on the same. I may be contacted at 876-222-2222 or Sblack21@gmail.com. Thank you in advance.

Yours sincerely,
  T. Campbell
  Trecia Campbell

Letter of Request Sample #2

Capital Heights
Green Pond
Montego Bay #1 P.O.
St. James

April 14, 2024

Mrs. Stacy Clarke-Huie
The Manager
ABC Call Centre Limited
Orange Hill
Montego Bay
St. James

Dear Mrs. Clarke-Huie,

<u>RE: Character Reference</u>

This is a formal request for a character and capability reference on my behalf. If you were able to attest to my qualifications for employment, and the skills I attained during my tenure at ABC Company, I would sincerely appreciate it.

I am in the process of seeking employment and a positive reference from you would enhance my prospects of achieving my career goals.

Please let me know if there is any information regarding my experience that I may provide to assist you with providing the reference. I may be reached at jsmith@abcd.com or 876- 111- 1111.

Thank you in advance.

Sincerely,

__R. Hemmings___
Ricardo Hemmings

Letter of Request Activities

Question 1: You are Melecia Wright, a 6th grade teacher at Riverside Primary School, which is located at 77 Riverside Drive, St. James. Your class has performed exceptionally well in their end-of-term exams in June 2024 when they were in grade 5. You would like to reward them with a trip to Dunn's River Falls in Ocho Rios, St. Ann. Write a letter to the principal, Mr. Javion Williams, requesting permission to organize the trip. Be sure to include all the necessary details.

Question 2: You name is Kesanique Reid, the president of the Student Council at Hillside High School, which is located at 77 Hillside Drive, St. James. The council is planning a fundraising event to support the needy students at the school. You need to request the use of the school's auditorium for the event, scheduled for September 20, 2024. Write a letter to the principal, Mrs. Mya Simpson-Cato, asking for permission to use the auditorium, and explain how the event will be organized.

Question 3: You were a student at the University of the West Indies, Mona, but you migrated to the USA and transferred to another university. You now need to request a transcript from UWI to complete your records at your current institution, Florida State University. Write a letter of request to the Registrar's Office at UWI, explaining the situation, providing your full name, student ID, and programme of study, and any other pertinent information. Also, request that the transcript to be sent directly to Florida State University's Admissions Office. The addresses for both universities are below.

University of the West Indies, Mona Campus	Admissions Office
Registrar's Office	Florida State University
University of the West Indies, Mona	282 Champions Way,
Mona, Kingston 7	Tallahassee, FL 32306
Jamaica	USA

Letter to the Editor

A **Letter to the Editor** may be written to the editor of a newspaper or a magazine. It is written to highlight a social issue or problem. It can also be written in order to get it published in the said medium. As it is a **formal letter,** the format has to be followed strictly. Only formal language can be used i.e., abbreviations and slang language should be avoided.

The format of a letter to the editor of a newspaper is as follows:
1. **Sender's address**: The address and contact details of the sender are written here. **(THIS IS OPTIONAL FOR THE SENDER. EVEN IF IT IS INCLUDED, THE NEWSPAPER DOES NOT PUBLISH IT).**
2. **Date:** The date is written below the sender's address after leaving one space or line.
3. **Receiving Editor's address**: The address of the recipient of the mail i.e. the editor is written here.
4. **Subject of the letter**: The main purpose of the letter forms the subject. It must be written in one line. It must convey the matter for which the letter is written.
5. **Salutation** (Sir / Respected sir / Madam/Dear Editor)
6. **Body:** The matter of the letter is written here. It is divided into 3 or more paragraphs as follows
   - **Opening Paragraph:** Introduce yourself and the purpose of writing the letter in brief.
   - **Body Paragraphs**: Give details of the matter.
   - **Closing Paragraph:** Conclude by mentioning what you expect from the editor. (For example, you may want him to highlight the issue in his newspaper/magazine).
7. **Complimentary Closing.**
8. **Sender's name and/or signature, and designation** (if any). Some senders do not use their full name, they may use an alias, their initials, or a phrase such as "Concerned Citizen."

Sample #1 (with sender's address and the date and the inside address)

Cambridge P.O.
St. James

November 23, 2021

Ms. Lorian Shaw
The Editor
The Western Mirror
12 Union Street
Montego Bay
St. James

THE EDITOR, Madam:

Workers negatively impacted by COVID-19

A study on the impact of COVID-19 on Jamaican workers yielded some insightful results. A sample of ,1057 workers from various private- and public-sector companies participated in a cross-sectional survey conducted by the Hugh Shearer Labour Studies Institute and the Ministry of Labour and Social Security. The findings indicated that most participants (90.3 per cent) were sufficiently educated about the pandemic. However, males (92.1 per cent) were more educated about the pandemic, compared to females (89.6 per cent).

Participants also indicated that their employers were using various strategies to respond to the pandemic. Based on the responses, participants believed that employers were using flexible working hours, layoffs, redundancies, wage cuts, reducing working hours, and freezing benefits and commissions to respond to the number of issues caused by the pandemic.

A sizable number of the sample negatively when asked if they were coping well with the pandemic. The findings showed that most males indicated that they were coping very well with the pandemic in comparison to females Most respondents did not believe that their employers were sufficiently prepared for COVID-19. The data showed that more than half of the sample did not agree that their employers were sufficiently prepared for the pandemic. A noticeable number of participants from the private sector (23.2 percent) strongly disagreed that their company was prepared for COVID-19.

LAUREN MARSH
Acting Head, Hugh Shearer
Labour Studies Institute
University of the West Indies,
Open Campus
Available at: https://jamaica-gleaner.com/article/letters/20211123/letter-day-workers-negatively-impacted-covid-19

Sample #2 (without the sender's address and the inside address).

July 30, 2024

Dear Editor,

CXC is at it Again!

The Caribbean Examinations Council (CXC) is at it again! It is not news that CXC has decided to discontinue agricultural science (double option), mechanical engineering, green engineering as well as electrical and electronic technology. Notice came to the education system across the region in a Nicodemus nature overnight. Dr Wayne Wesley, CEO of CXC, identified low registration and the corresponding economic cost to offer these subjects as the rationale for their discontinuation.

Who did CXC consult about this discontinuation? CXC has a propensity to confuse consultation with sensitisation. We are in a sad state of affairs, as CXC appears to report to no one! It is judge, jury, and executioner on all matters relating to the assessment of our students and it does so with impunity and a total lack of regard for key players and clients, such as students, parents, teachers, and possible governments in the region. CXC must be democratised with urgency and not only transform but reform itself to reflect an organisation that is innovative, collaborative, flexible, and credible.

Additionally, what are the implications of discontinuing these subjects for the STEAM (science, technology, engineering, arts, mathematics) thrust in the region? The proposed saving grace is that the territories that wish to offer these subjects can do so but must be prepared to foot the full economic cost. To date, of note, we have not heard from the policymakers in the region on such an important matter. Should we as the public take it that our policymakers are suffering from amnesia, or is it a case that they support this debilitating move by CXC? We deserve to hear from them, as the silence is deafening and palpable.

As a region we must be concerned about this decision and its impact on the advancement of science, technology, and economic growth and development in the region. The potential reduction in the pool of talent going into electronics and scientific inquiry can lead to skill gaps for the fields of mechanics, civil and electrical engineering, and agriculture which will significantly impact our global competitiveness.

Consequently, there must be a review of the decision to ensure we provide people with the skill set necessary to meet the needs of our region. We must, as educators and citizens in general, save CXC from itself and, by extension, our region.

Garth Anderson
President, Caribbean Union of Teachers
Principal, Church Teachers' College
Available at: https://www.jamaicaobserver.com/2024/05/23/cxc-is-at-it-again/

Letter to the Editor Activities

Question 1: You live in a community where the roads have been in poor condition for years, leading to damage to vehicles and causing significant inconvenience to residents. Write a letter to the editor of The Jamaica Gleaner, Mr. Kirkton Bennett, highlighting the issue of the deteriorating roads in your area, urging the authorities to take immediate action.

Address the letter to: Mr. Kirkton Bennett
The Editor
The Jamaica Gleaner
7 North Street
Kingston
Jamaica

Question 2: You are concerned about the issue of gender pay inequality in Jamaica, where women are often paid less than men for doing the same job. Write a letter to the editor of The Jamaica Observer, Mr. Chris-al Erickson, to voice your concerns and call for stronger measures to ensure that both men and women receive equal pay for equal work.

Address the letter to:
Mr. Chris-al Erickson
The Editor
The Jamaica Observer
40-42 ½ Beechwood Avenue
Kingston 5, Jamaica

Question 3: The crime rate in Jamaica has been a growing concern, with increasing incidents of violence and theft affecting communities across the country. Write a letter to the editor of The Sunday Herald, Mr. Damian Robinson, expressing your thoughts on the rising crime rates and suggesting solutions that could help make the country safer.

Address the letter to:
Mr. Damian Robinson
The Editor
The Sunday Herald
32 Constant Spring Road
Kingston 10
Jamaica

The Simple Report

A report is a structured document that provides information on a specific topic, event, or situation. It is usually written to inform, explain or analyze a situation. Reports are commonly used in academic, professional, and organizational settings and typically include factual data presented in a clear and organized manner.

Types of Reports

- Simple Report (For Example: Eyewitness Report and Second-Hand Account Report).

- Newspaper Report

- Evaluation Report

- Field Report

The Simple Report

A simple report is a basic or brief form of a report that focuses on passing on essential information without unnecessary details or complexity. It is concise and easy to understand, making it suitable for straightforward topics or smaller tasks. The two simple reports that will be discussed are the **eyewitness report,** and the **second-hand account report.**

FEATURES OF A SIMPLE REPORT

- **A simple report should relate factual information** – opinions or biases are not expressed. Be objective.

- **Length-** A simple report is shorter than a comprehensive report as it only focuses on essential details. For CXC, the length is 200 to 250 words.

- **Content-** A simple report focuses on one main topic or issue.

- **Language-** The language should be simple and clear.

- **Format-** Logical arrangement is necessary. There must be some order for the report. It must be in paragraph form. Longer reports might be divided into subheadings to show development. Some reports might go from the most important point to the least important. Simple reports follow chronological order; information is arranged in the manner it occurs. E.g. First…after…then…

- **Have clarity** – In a simple report, simple straightforward language is used. It should be easy to understand what is being related.

- **Be concise** – Only relevant information should be given. If the information is not directly related to what happened, eliminate it.

- **Be precise**- get to the point.

FORMAT OF THE SIMPLE REPORT

For CSEC purposes, the focus will be on the letter writing format.

LETTER WRITING FORMAT

The block letter writing format is used. This format follows the regular outline for business letters. The parts of the business letter as listed below are usually used.

1) **Sender's Address:**
   - Located at the top of the letter, typically aligned to the left.

2) **Date:**
   - Placed below the sender's address. It is aligned with it.
   - It's important to ensure the date is current and accurate.

3) **Inside Address:**
   - This is the recipient's address. It is placed below the date.
   - It includes the recipient's name, title, company, and company's street address.
   - It's important to use the correct title and address.

4) **Salutation:**
   - A greeting to the recipient, placed after the inside address.
   - Common salutations include: "Dear Mr./Ms. [followed by the persons last name]" or "Dear Sir/Madam" (if the recipient's name is unknown).
   - Always use a colon (:) after the salutation in the report.

5) **Subject:**
   - A short line that summarizes the purpose or topic of the report. It is placed below the salutation (often in bold and caps).
   - It should not be a complete sentence.

6) **Body:**
   - The main content of the report where the purpose is explained clearly.
   - It should be well-organized into short paragraphs for readability.
   - The tone should be formal, professional, and polite.

7) **Closing:**
   - A formal way to end the report. It is placed after the body.
   - Some common closings are: "Sincerely," "Best regards," or "Yours faithfully."
   - Only the first word in the closing should start with a capital letter.

8) **Signature:**
   - The sender's handwritten signature should be placed below the closing.
   - The sender's full name (and title if necessary) is usually typed below the signature.

EYEWITNESS REPORT

An eyewitness report is a written or verbal account of an event or incident, provided by someone who personally observed it happen. It is typically factual and focused on describing what occurred, who was involved, and when and where it happened. This type of report is often used in situations such as accidents, crimes, or any significant event where an observer's account is valuable for documentation or investigation.

KEY FEATURES OF AN EYEWITNESS REPORT

1. **Firsthand Account**: Written from the perspective of someone who directly witnessed the event.
2. **Factual Details**: Focuses on facts, not opinions or assumptions.
3. **Chronological Order**: Events are described in the order they occurred.
4. **Specific Details**: Includes **who, what, when, where, and how** of the incident.
5. **Objectivity**: Avoids bias, emotions, or speculation

AN EXAMPLE OF AN EYEWITNESS REPORT

2 Blueberry Street
Montego Bay #2 P.O.
St. James

August 26, 2024

Ms. Journey McIntosh
The Form Teacher: Grade 9-2
St. James High School
2 Orange Street
Montego Bay #1 P.O.
St. James

Dear Ms. McIntosh,

RE: BROKEN WINDOW IN GRADE 9-2

    This is a formal report of an incident I witnessed on Wednesday, August 26, 2024. at approximately 12:15 p.m. in the grade 9-2 classroom. The window beside the cupboard was broken by a ball while the students from grade 9-2 were engaged in a game of cricket. Marvia McKenzie accidentally hit the ball in the window while they were playing.

It was lunch time, and it was raining heavily. I saw the students moved all the benches to the left side of the classroom to play a game of cricket on the right side of the classroom. My friends and I decided not to participate in the game, so we sat at the back of the classroom to have our lunches. As the form captain, I warned the students not to engage in a cricket game indoors as the space was too small and it was risky. However, they ignored me. At one point they got so noisy, that Ms. Angella Findlater from grade 9-1 came by and broke up the game. However, as soon as Ms. Findlater left, they started playing again.

At approximately 12: 15 p.m. I heard a loud crash which was followed by screams from the students. The window by the cupboard was shattered and glass and splinters were all over the classroom. I saw when Crystal Scott threw the ball, and then Marvia McKenzie hit the ball which went directly into the window and smashed it. The students who were playing shouted at each other and blamed each other for the incident.

The noise and shouting caused an uproar on the grade 9 block as other teachers and students came by to see what took place. Marvia started to cry because everyone put all the blame on her. Ms. Findlater came by again and reprimanded all the students involved. She spoke firmly to them about disobedience and respecting authority, as she had warned them earlier to stop the game. She took all the students involved to the principal's office. I went along with them. After inquiring what happened, the principal Mr. Nicholas Hamilton, decided that all the students involved were responsible for the damage. The principal called the parents of all the students who were playing. He told each parent the amount of money he/she had to pay to get the window replaced. The students involved were each given one week of detention to clean the schoolyard after school every day. They will also apologize to the entire school population at the general devotion on Monday, August 30, 2024.

Yours truly,
__K. Mundle__
Kadine Mundle
Form Captain

Eyewitness Report Activities

Activity 1: Write a simple report to your form teacher Mrs. Malcolm-Blackwood detailing a fight you witnessed between the physical education teacher, Mr. Lanzel Stewart, and Joavid Rose from grade 9S, on Wednesday, August 14, 2024, during physical education class. Address the report to:

Mrs. Malcolm-Blackwood
The Form Teacher: 9S
Rose Park High School

Rose Street
Montego Bay
St. James

Activity 2: Write a simple report describing an argument you witnessed between two managers at Oceanview Resort. The managers names are Dejonae Mckenzie and Rodney Dobson. The argument occurred in front of guests on Friday, August 16, 2024. Include details about the context of the argument, the managers involved, and how it affected the guests. Address the report to:

Mr. Deshawn McKenzie
General Manager
Oceanview Resort
12 Beachside Drive
Negril
Westmoreland

Activity 3: Write a simple report about a vehicular accident you witnessed on the hill at St. James High School on Tuesday, August 20, 2024. Two teachers, Ms. Breshawna McKenzie and Mr. Ricardo Harding were involved in the accident. Detail what happened, who was involved, and any actions taken afterward, such as calling for help or assisting the injured. Address the report to:
Mr. Joseph Williams
The Principal
St. James High School
Orange Hill
Montego Bay
St. James

SECOND-HAND ACCOUNT REPORT

A second-hand account report is a written account of an event, incident, or situation based on information provided by others rather than directly witnessing or experiencing it yourself. This type of report relies on details communicated to the writer by eyewitnesses, participants, or other sources.

KEY FEATURES OF A SECOND-HAND ACCOUNT REPORT

1. **Indirect Observation:** The writer did not witness the event but is compiling the report based on what was reported to them.

2. **Attribution:** The report should make it clear that the information comes from other individuals or sources. Some phrases that may be used are, "I was told," "According to witnesses," and "Based on the accounts provided".
3. **Accuracy and Objectivity:** It relies on faithfully recording the information received without adding personal bias or assumptions.
4. **Clarity and Detail:** The report should include the key facts of the incident, such as who was involved, what happened, where and when it occurred, and its impact.

AN EXAMPLE OF A SECOND-HAND ACCOUNT REPORT

2 Blueberry Street
Montego Bay #2 P.O.
St. James

August 26, 2024

Ms. Karel Shaw
The Form Teacher: Grade 9-2
St. James High School
2 Orange Street
Montego Bay #1 P.O.
St. James

Dear Ms. Shaw,

RE: BROKEN WINDOW IN GRADE 9-2

This is a formal report based on information I received regarding an incident that occurred on Wednesday, August 26, 2024, at approximately 12:15 p.m. in the grade 9-2 classroom. I was informed by Sandra Thomas, the assistant form captain, that the window beside the cupboard was broken by a ball during a cricket game played by students of grade 9-2. According to reports from the Sandra, the incident happened when Marvia McKenzie accidentally hit the ball into the window.

I was told that this happened during the lunch break when it was raining heavily. The students reportedly moved all the benches to the left side of the classroom to make space for playing cricket on the right side. Some students chose not to participate and instead sat at the back of the room to have their lunches. Sandra said she warned the students against playing cricket indoors, citing the limited space and the risks involved. However, the students ignored the warning and continued with their game.

She said that at one point, the game became so noisy that Ms. Angella Findlater, a teacher from grade 9-1, intervened and instructed the students to stop playing. However, as soon as Ms.

Findlater left, the students resumed their game. At approximately 12:15 p.m., a loud crash was heard, followed by screams. Upon investigation, it was found that the window near the cupboard had shattered, leaving glass and splinters scattered across the classroom.

Students who were playing cricket reportedly began shouting and blaming each other for the incident. Sandra revealed that Crystal Scott had thrown the ball, and Marvia McKenzie had hit it, causing the ball to crash into the window. The commotion attracted the attention of other students and teachers on the grade 9 block, who came to see what had happened.

Marvia McKenzie reportedly became emotional and started crying as the other students blamed her for the damage. Ms. Findlater returned to the scene, reprimanded all the students involved, and spoke to them about disobedience and respecting authority, reminding them of her earlier warning. She then escorted the students to the principal's office. Sandra said she went along with them.

It was reported that after he inquired about the incident, the principal, Mr. Nicholas Hamilton, determined that all students involved in the game were responsible for the damage. He contacted their parents, informing them of the costs for replacing the window. Additionally, the students were assigned one week of detention to clean the schoolyard after school and were required to apologize publicly during the general devotion on Monday, August 30, 2024.

Yours truly,
__T. Samuels__
Torrey Samuels
Assistant Form Captain

Second-Hand Account Report Activities

Activity 1: You are the assistant to the General Manager at Oceanview Resort. On Friday, December 13, 2024, a staff member, Creg Parker, reported to you that two managers, Dejonae McKenzie and Rodney Dobson, were involved in a heated argument in the lobby area. The argument occurred in full view of guests and disrupted the atmosphere. You were told that the argument stemmed from a disagreement about task delegation for an upcoming event. Creg Parker mentioned that the managers raised their voices, and some guests appeared uncomfortable or upset. Write a formal report to the General Manager, based on the information provided to you about the argument between the two managers. Be sure to include details about the managers involved, the context of the argument, and its impact on guests and staff. Address the report to:

Dr. Reginea Shirley
The General Manager
Oceanview Resort
1905 Turks Avenue

Cornwall Courts
Montego Bay
St. James.

Activity 2: You are a student at Eastview Secondary School. On Tuesday, December 17, 2024, during lunchtime, a fellow student, Rushel-lee Bell, reported to you that she witnessed a fight between two teachers, Ms. Monique Robinson and Mr. Taimar McIntosh, in the staffroom. According to Rushel-lee Bell, the fight started after an argument over a misunderstanding about the grading system for the upcoming semester. She mentioned that the teachers were raising their voices, and other staff members seemed uncomfortable. Other students who were in the staffroom reported feeling awkward due to the tension. Write a formal report to the principal, based on the information provided to you about the incident involving the two teachers. Be sure to include the teachers' names, the nature of the disagreement, and its impact on the staff and students. Address the report to:

Ms. Samantha Morris
The Principal
Eastview Secondary School
Bethel Town P.O.
Westmoreland

Activity 3: You are a student at Greenfield High School. On Wednesday, December 18, 2024, a fellow student, Dean Thomas, reported to you that he witnessed a bullying incident between two students, Sonya Nelson and Noelia Knock, in the schoolyard. Dean explained that Noelia had been teasing Sonya about her appearance in front of a group of other students. According to Dean, Noelia's comments were hurtful, and Sonya appeared upset, though she did not respond verbally. Dean also mentioned that other students laughed, making Sonya feel isolated. Write a formal report to the school counsellor, based on the information provided to you about the bullying incident. Address the report to:

Mr. Aaron Hall
The Guidance Counsellor
Greenfield High School
Cambridge P.O.
St. James

The Newspaper Report

News:

News is newly received or noteworthy information, especially about recent events.

Five (5) Characteristics of News

The major characteristics of news are as follow. News should be:

(a) Accurate
(b) Balanced
(c) Objective
(d) Concise (and clear)
(e) Current

The key elements of a Newspaper Report are:

1. Headline

- Catches your attention
- Sums up the story
- Should be a short and eye-catching phrase (it should not be a full sentence)
- Should be in bold and all caps

2. Byline

- Writer's name
- Writer's Specialty, e.g., sports, food, crime, current events
- The date

3. Placeline

- Where the story begins.
- Gives the place where the incident in the story took place

4. Lead

- The opening section
- Gives most important information
- Should answer most of the 5 W's

5. Body

- Supplies details
- Most important details come first
- Simple true statements are used

6. Quotation

- What someone actually said (must be in quotation marks)

- Adds accuracy
- Adds an "at the scene" feeling

Newspaper Report – Example 1
AGAINST ALL ODDS

June 6, 2018

Melonie Richards & Sandrae Vincent

Youth Sportswriters

Sydney Australia: Christopher Brodie is this morning celebrating his gold medal success in the Paralympics 100m sprint. Yesterday, in the packed stadium in Sydney, Australia, where the games have been taking place all week, Chris ran the race of his life to cross the line in the gold medal position.

For any athlete a championship medal is the ultimate achievement, but for Chris it was also the culmination of years of determination and courage. The 20-year-old was just 5 when he had to have his right leg amputated below the knee. The pain caused by his artificial leg was not enough to stop the lively youngster from Motherwell running around living life to the full.

When he joined the local athletics club, he never dreamt that he would end up an Olympic champion.

Now, thanks to the pioneering work of sports scientists and the doctors at Glasgow's St Thomas' Hospital, Chris has been able to take advantage of the latest sports technology, a new prosthetic sports leg.

"The new leg is made of lightweight materials, and the foot section has as close to normal foot movement as an artificial leg can get," said Ken Brown, one of the doctors who worked on the project. Chris backed up Dr. Brown's claim when he said that the new leg allowed for fluid movement and a much less cumbersome running style.

Certainly, the benefits the artificial leg will bring to sports women and men all over the world could be seen yesterday in Sydney, when Chris Brodie showed the world what a powerful combination courage and innovation can be.

Can you identify the WHO, WHAT, WHERE, WHEN, WHY and HOW in this news report?

a) Who is the main person the story is about?
b) What has happened to him?
c) Where did the event take place?
d) When did it happen?

e) Why did it happen?

  f) How did it take place?

Example #2

CAR THIEF TRAPPED IN TARGET VEHICLE (headline)

May 13, 2019 **(byline)**

Creg Parker & Kristina Shiley **(byline)**

Intern Youth Reporters **(byline)**

(Placeline) Reuters, Australia- **(Lead)** A bungling Australian car thief was nabbed after accidentally locking himself in the vehicle he was trying to steal, police said Wednesday.

(Body) Police were called to a house in Adelaide after two thieves were heard trying to steal a car. On arrival they were surprised to find a 53-year-old man hiding inside the vehicle. The man was identified as Bentley Reid of Southside Sydney Australia

"The man, while breaking into the car, had locked himself in the car and couldn't get out," **(quotation)** South Australian police said, adding a second thief was found hiding in nearby bushes.

"It is the most bizarre incident we have seen for a while in our community," one resident who identified himself as Haydn Wishart said. "Nothing like this ever happens in Adelaide, we are glad God allowed things to work out the way it did, and the car was not stolen."

Both men were later taken into police custody. The Adelaide Police Department is investigating

Newspaper Report Activity

Use the headlines below to write newspaper stories.

a) Man Falls to His Death in Greenpond

b) Salt Spring Residents Protest for Better Roads

c) Mid-day Shooting at Sam Sharpe Square

d) Child Hero Saves Drowning Old Woman

e) Ward of the State Achieves 15 Grades Ones in CXC

f) Montego Bay Mayor on the Run

g) Extreme Heat Causes Schools to Close

Blogs

A blog is a website or virtual journal where users share their ideas, reflections, and writings on various subjects. It is frequently updated, and the tone of the text is typically casual or informal.

Basic Blog Characteristics:

(a) **Frequent Updates**: New posts are frequently added to blogs on a daily, weekly, or monthly basis.

(b) **Informal Tone**: The writing is typically conversational and informal.

(c) **Personal or Professional:** Blogs can include both professional and personal perspectives and experiences.

(d) **Comments Section**: A lot of blogs let users leave comments and communicate with the writers.

(e) **Post-by-Post Arrangement**: Articles are uploaded from newest to oldest in reverse chronological sequence.

Types of Blogs:

1. **Personal Blogs**: Focus on an individual's experiences, hobbies, or interests.

2. **Business Blogs**: Written by companies to provide information related to their products or services.

3. **Niche Blogs**: Centred around a specific topic like travel, food, fitness, or technology.

4. **News Blogs**: Cover the latest events and updates in a specific area, like current events or a particular industry.

5. **Lifestyle Blogs**: Cover a broad range of topics like fashion, health, and relationships.

Blog Sample

---

http://www.mymixedblogspot.com

The Value of Consistent Exercise by Richanda Shaw- November 30, 2024

Maintaining an active lifestyle is crucial for mental and physical health. Exercise improves general health rather than merely helping people gain muscle or lose weight. Frequent exercise can improve your mood, give you more energy, and help you live a longer, healthier life. Getting some sort of exercise each day is essential, whether it's a vigorous workout, a yoga session, or a quick stroll in the morning.

The beneficial effects of exercise on mental health are among its biggest advantages. Endorphins are brain chemicals released during physical activity that have the dual benefits of improving mood and acting as natural painkillers. Accordingly, regular exercise can aid in lowering tension,

> anxiety, and even depressive symptoms. Even on my busiest days, I've found that taking even 20 minutes to stretch or go for a walk helps me decompress and feel more energised.
>
> The largest obstacle for a lot of individuals is finding time to exercise. When things become busy in life, it's simple to put fitness last on your list of priorities. But the secret is to start with small, doable adjustments. Start with something easy, like a quick workout at home in the morning or a 10-minute stroll after supper, rather than striving for hour-long gym sessions every day. These tiny actions might develop into enduring routines.
>
> Regular exercise also has a positive impact on physical health. It can reduce the risk of chronic illnesses like diabetes and high blood pressure and strengthen the heart and circulation. Exercise can also help with weight management and enhance the quality of sleep.
>
> An integral aspect of leading a balanced and healthy life is regular exercise. It improves your emotional and physical well-being, making you feel happier and more energised. The secret is constancy; even little, regular efforts can add up to big things. Choose a hobby or pastime you enjoy, then get going!
>
> **NB: All comments are welcomed.**

Blog Activities

Activity 1: Write a blog post describing several popular tourist attractions in Jamaica. Highlight places like Dunn's River Falls, Blue Hole, Mystic Mountain, and Negril's Seven Mile Beach. Explain what makes each attraction unique and why tourists from around the world are drawn to these locations.

Activity 2: Write a blog post about the variety of delicious Jamaican foods. Discuss popular dishes such as jerk chicken, curry goat, oxtail, and festival. Mention traditional favourites like ackee and saltfish, along with snacks such as patties and bammies.

Activity 3: Pretend you are world traveller named Xavier James who has visited several countries. Write a blog post describing some of the places you've explored abroad. Share your experiences visiting cities like Paris, New York, Tokyo, or Rome. Talk about the unique cultures, food, landmarks, and memorable moments you had in each place.

Minutes

A meeting's decisions, discussions, and actions are documented in writing in the minutes. They act as a formal record, summarizing the main issues raised, choices made, and steps that need to be done. They are necessary to guarantee accountability and monitor development.

Components of Good Minutes
1. **Heading**
    - o The organization or meeting name
    - o The meeting's date, time, and place

- o The names of those in attendance and those who are not
- o The name of the person presiding over the assembly
- o The name of the individual recording minutes

2. **Call to Order**
   - o The time the meeting was declared open
   - o Who declared the meeting open?

3. **Approval of Previous Minutes**
   - o A statement regarding the approval, modification, or correction of the minutes from the prior meeting.

4. **Reports**
   - o Reports that committee chairs or individual presenters summarize.
   - o Include pertinent information, decisions, and any necessary actions.

5. **Discussions and Decisions**
   - o Major topics covered in the meeting.
   - o Main topics of discussion, participants, and noteworthy viewpoints or recommendations.
   - o All decisions (motions approved or denied) must be documented, along with the names of the proposer and the seconder.

6. **Action Items**
   - o Particular assignments made at the meeting, together with who is in charge of them and when they are due.
   - o Information on any necessary follow-up steps.

7. **New Business**
   - o An overview of newly brought up issues, decisions made, and actions postponed

8. **Adjournment**
   - o The closing time of the meeting.
   - o Closing remarks

9. **Next Meeting**
   - o The next meeting's date, time, and place (if determined).

10. **Signature**
    - o The minutes' approval (often confirmed at the following meeting) and the name and signature of the person who took them.

Sample Minutes

Minutes of ABC Company Team Meeting
Date: August 11, 2024
Time: 10:00 AM
Location: Conference Room, ABC Headquarters

Robert Shirley declared the meeting open at 10:05 AM. Robert Shirley (Chairman), Anthony Shirley (Secretary), Alice Brown, and Xavier James were present. Mark Green was not present. Without any changes, the minutes of the August 20, 2024, prior meeting were examined and approved.

The finance report was given by Alice Brown, who also mentioned that the company's expenses had decreased by 5% and its revenue had climbed by 10% from the previous quarter. Regarding the report, there were none. Next, Xavier James gave a plan for the marketing strategy for Q4. After deliberation, a $10,000 increase in the campaign budget was decided upon. The motion was approved unanimously after Alice Brown made the initial move and Robert Shirley seconded it.

Two action items were assigned: Xavier James will complete the marketing plan and submit it for review by September 20, 2024, and Alice Brown will update the budget and present it by September 15, 2024. The meeting saw no new business brought up. The next meeting is set for September 30, 2024, at 10:00 AM in the same place. The meeting was adjourned at 11:30 AM.

Regards,

Anthony Shirley
Secretary

Minutes Activities

Activity 1: Write the minutes for your school's student council meeting held on September 1, 2024, at 3:00 p.m. The meeting was held to plan an upcoming school event (a charity concert). Include discussions about the event date, budget, promotion, and roles assigned to student council members. Note any decisions made regarding venue, performers, and ticket prices.

Activity 2: Write the minutes for a youth meeting at your church held on September 5, 2024, at 5:00 p.m. The meeting was focused on planning a surprise pastoral anniversary celebration for the bishops. The bishops' names are Gifford Shaw and Craig Marshall. Include key discussions about the event date, venue, theme, and assignments for organizing decorations, invitations, and food.

Activity 3: Write the minutes for XYZ Company meeting held on August 25, 2024, at 10:00 a.m. The meeting was about the company's plans to improve employee attendance and to discuss ideas for the staff end-of-year party. Include the date, time, who was at the meeting, and the main things that were talked about or decided.

Emails

No matter what industry they work in, a lot of people read and write emails for many hours of the day. Email, short for electronic mail, is one of the main methods of business communication. Before writing an effective email, the sender must determine whether email is the right communication medium. Emails ought to be brief and direct. Only those who truly need to see them should receive them, and the sender should be very explicit about the next action they would like the recipient to take. One's professionalism, morals, and attention to detail are all reflected in their emails.

How to Write an Excellent Email

1. Limit your email correspondence. Do not over communicate.
2. Utilize the subject lines effectively.
3. Make messages concise and unambiguous.
4. Use simple, clear language
5. Show courtesy.
6. Pay attention to your tone.
7. Proofread before you send.

CC and BCC

The acronyms BCC and CC are options that your email application will display. The acronym for carbon copy is CC. You utilize it when you wish to communicate with interested parties in addition to the primary recipient. It will be visible to others that you sent the email to another person. Sometimes you might want a message to remain private and not be shown to everyone. Then, you would type their email addresses in the "blind carbon copy," or BCC, area.

Sample Email

From: seniorsecretary@acbcompany.com

To: ceo@acbcompany.com

CC: seniormanager@acbcompany.com

BCC: eventplanning@acbcompany.com

Date: August 15, 2024

Subject: Surprise Retirement Dinner for Mr. Adrian McLennon

Dear Mr. Brown,

    I trust this email finds you well. I would like to inform you about a wonderful celebration we have planned for Mr. McLennon, a longtime and devoted employee of ACB Group. He will be retiring at the end of August 2024, after 35 years of exceptional service to the business.

    We are very grateful for his unshakable commitment and outstanding services, and to show our appreciation, we are hosting a surprise retirement luncheon in his honour. The event will take place in the Kensington Hotel's Grand Ballroom on Friday, August 23, 2024, starting at 6:00 PM. We hope that many friends, senior management, and coworkers will join us, making it a special evening for Mr. McLennon.

> As we acknowledge that Mr. McLennon's commitment and leadership have been essential to ACB Group's success throughout the years, we would be genuinely honoured if you could join us in honouring his extraordinary career. This great moment would be even more significant with your presence.
>
> If there are any other ways you think we can make this evening even more memorable, please don't hesitate to suggest them. We hope to see you there and eagerly await your confirmation.
>
> Kind regards,
>
> Jay-Ann Irving Miller
> Senior Secretary
> 876-000-0000

Email Activities

Activity 1: Write an email to your principal, Mr. Lamar Christie asking for permission to host an end-of-year class party for your grade. His email address is principal@roseparkgighschool.edu.jm. Be sure to explain why it would be a fun and memorable way to celebrate the end of the school year. Suggest possible dates, locations, activities, and other pertinent information. As the sender, use your own email address.

Activity 2: Write an email to your manager, Mr. Johnathan Schloss suggesting that the company should expand its operations and hire more employees. Explain how the business is growing, and why it's necessary to bring in more staff to keep up with the demand. Send the email to: jschloss@freshgrocerystore.com. Also, send a CC of the email to the assistant manager Ms. Adonia Ferguson. Her email address is assistantmanager@freshgrocerystore.com. As the sender, use your own email address.

Activity 3: Write an email to Mrs. Jennifer Schloss, the manager of Ocean Breeze Resort, explaining the problems you encountered during your recent stay. Mention issues such as poor customer service, dirty rooms, malfunctioning amenities and any other problems you faced. Be sure to include how disappointed you were and what you expect as a resolution. Send the email to: manager@oceanbreezeresort.com. Also send a BCC to the assistant manager Mr. Dante Pryce. His email address is assistantmanager@ceanbreezeresort.com. As the sender, use your own email address

Memorandum / Memo

A Memorandum, also called "memo, is a form of written communication that is usually used within an organization to disseminate information, issue announcements, or offer updates. Although it is not as formal as a letter, it is nonetheless used as an official document to notify team members or employees of particular policies, events, or issues. Memos are perfect for internal communication since they are brief, understandable, and direct.

What Makes a Memorandum?

1. **Heading:** Contains the word "Memorandum" or "Memo" at the top and all pertinent information, such as the sender, recipient, date, and subject.
2. **Recipient:** The recipient of a memo is the person to whom it is addressed, such as department heads or employees.
3. **Sender:** The memo's sender indicates who is sending it.
4. **Date:** Indicates the memo's issue date.
5. **Subject:** Gives a short summary of the memo's contents.
6. **Introduction:** Gives background information or context at the outset and explains the memo's goal.
7. **Body:** Describes in further detail any necessary decisions, directions, or activities.
8. **Conclusion:** This section may include a summary of the main ideas or demand a particular action, such as acknowledging receipt of the memo or attending an event.
9. **Signature:** Although official signatures are not usually required, the sender's name or initials are sometimes included to show authenticity.

Sample Memorandum
ACB Company

Memorandum
To: All Employees
From: [Crystal Dobson], Human Resources Manager
Date: August 10, 2024
Subject: Volunteer Visit to Infirmary

Dear Team,

We are happy to inform that, as part of our volunteer program, ACB Company will be visiting the XYZ Infirmary on Saturday, August 24, 2024, from 9:00 AM to 2:00 PM. Meal serving, socializing with the inhabitants, and supplying necessities are all part of the activities.

Please let us know by August 17, 2024, if you are willing to volunteer. When the event gets closer, more information will be released.

We appreciate your help in supporting community camaraderie and development.

Best regards,

C. Dobson
Human Resources Manager

Memorandum Activities

Activity 1: You are Kayla Schloss, the principal of Stars Basic School. Write a memo to the staff informing them about an upcoming visit to a local children's home. Include details such as the date, time, location, and purpose of the visit. Encourage everyone to participate.

Activity 2: You are Mr. Richard Miller, the manager of XYZ Shipping Company. Write a memo to your colleagues informing them about an important staff meeting. Be sure to include the date, time, location, and topics that will be discussed.

Activity 3: Write a memo to the staff of Shirley's Institute informing them about a planned staff outing to Kool Runnings Water Park in Westmoreland. Include details such as the date, meeting point, time of departure, and what to bring. Pretend you are Ms. Samoy S. Shirley, the principal of the institution.

Notices

An announcement in writing or print that alerts individuals to a certain decision, event, or piece of information is called a notice. To guarantee that the message reaches everyone in a timely manner, it is typically given to a certain audience or displayed in public. The tone of notices is concise, unambiguous, and formal.

Notice Format

a) **Title:** The word "NOTICE" at the top, bold and in capital.
b) **Date**: The day the notification was sent out.
c) **Heading:** A concise, identifiable heading that states the topic.
d) **Body**: the main material, +including vital data like time, date, venue, and any particular instructions.
e) **Issuer:** The name and status of the person or department issuing the notice.
f) **Signature**: The issuer's signature or initials (optional).

Sample Notice #1

NOTICE

Date: August 10, 2024

VOLUNTEER VISIT TO XYZ INFIRMARY

This is to inform all employees that ACB Company will be organizing a volunteer visit to the XYZ Infirmary on **Saturday, August 24, 2024**, from **9:00 AM to 2:00 PM**. Employees who wish to participate should confirm their attendance by **August 17, 2024**.

For further information, please contact the Human Resources Department.

Issued by: Ransford Stewart
Human Resources Manager

Sample Notice #2

NOTICE

Date: August 12, 2024

COOK-OUT FUNDRAISER

All employees are invited to a **Cook-Out Fundraiser** hosted by St. James High School Welfare Department on **Friday, August 16, 2024**, from **12:00 PM to 3:00 PM** in the St. James High School Auditorium. The proceeds will go toward supporting our students who are in need.

Menu and Prices:
- Jerk or Fried Chicken: $1500
- Escoveitch Fish: $2000
- Jerk Pork: $1700
- Sides include rice and peas, bammy, plantain, fried and roasted breadfruit, macaroni and cheese and potato salad.

Only CASH PAYMENTS will be accepted. We look forward to your support and participation.

Issued by:
Pamela Shaw-Rose
Events Coordinator

Notice Activities

Activity 1: You are Shanieka Lindsay, the events coordinator at Rose Park High School. Write a notice to inform the Rose Park High School community about an upcoming charity event to raise funds for the new auditorium. Include details such as the date, time, location, and how people can contribute or participate.

Activity 2: Write a notice informing students and staff of Little River High School about an upcoming food sale organized by the school's club. Provide details such as the date, time, location, and menu items that will be available for purchase. Pretend you are Mr. Aman Spence, the events coordinator.

Activity 3: Your name is Monique Robinson, and you are the coordinator of Freedom Tabernacle Apostolic Learning Institute. Write a notice informing the congregation of Freedom Tabernacle Apostolic Church about a special church service being held for the opening of the Freedom Tabernacle Apostolic Learning Institute. Include the date, time, venue, and any special guests or events planned for the service.

AGENDA

An agenda is a well-organized list of subjects, tasks, or things to be discussed, dealt with, or finished during a meeting or event. It acts as a road map, defining the goals, sequence of events, and time allotments to guarantee a successful and effective meeting.

PURPOSE OF AN AGENDA

1) **Meeting Guide**: An agenda serves to direct the meeting by giving it structure and guaranteeing that all significant subjects are covered.
2) **Time management**: An agenda prevents needless delays by allocating the proper amount of time for each topic.
3) **Preparation Tool**: An agenda assists participants in getting ready for the conversation.
4) **Clarity**: An agenda clearly states the goals and expectations of the meeting.

KEY ELEMENTS OF AN AGENDA

1. **Title:** Label as "Agenda" with the meeting name or event.
2. **Date and Time:** It should clearly state when the meeting will take place.
3. **Location:** It specifies the venue or include virtual meeting details.
4. **Participants:** The agenda lists attendees or groups involved.
5. **Objectives:** It summarizes the purpose of the meeting.
6. **Topics/Items:** It includes all topics to be covered, listed in order of priority.
7. **Timing:** Assign a time limit for each topic or segment.
8. **Facilitators:** It notes who will lead each discussion.
9. **Q&A/Discussion:** It allocates time for open discussions or questions.
10. **Closing Remarks:** It ends with a summary, action items, or next steps.

TIPS FOR AN EFFECTIVE AGENDA

1. **Be Particular**: Make use of succinct, unambiguous wording.
2. **Prioritize**: Set precedence by starting with the most important subjects.
3. **Structure Flexibility**: Provide a cushion against overruns (an overrun happens when a

meeting goes longer than schedule).

4. **Distribute Early**: To allow for preparation, distribute the agenda ahead of time.

SAMPLE AGENDA

St. James High School End-of-Year Staff Meeting Agenda

Date: [December 12, 2024]

Time: 9:00 AM - 2:30 PM

Location: [Audio Visual Room]

9:00 AM - 9:15 AM | Opening Prayer and Worship

Facilitator: Ms. Erica Barnett

- Prayer and worship to set the tone for the meeting.

9:15 AM - 9:30 AM | Welcome and Opening Remarks

Facilitator: Principal Nadia Robinson

- Overview of the agenda and objectives for the meeting.
- Acknowledgement of achievements and staff contributions.

9:30 AM - 10:00 AM | Review of School Year

Facilitator: Vice Principal Joan Chin

- Highlights and challenges of the academic year.
- Student achievements and areas for improvement.

10:00 AM - 10:30 AM | Department Reports

Facilitator: Various Department Heads

- Brief updates on department goals, outcomes, and reflections.
    - **Mathematics:** Ms. Nordia Robinson
    - **Science:** Ms. Shara-Lee Evans
    - **Language Arts:** Mrs. Debranette Mattis-Christie
    - **Social Studies:** Ms. Khava Hayles-Selby
    - **Special Education:** Ms. Tisananna Green

10:30 AM - 11:00 AM | Break

- Refreshments will be provided.

11:00 AM - 11:45 AM | Professional Development Review

Facilitator: Ms. Novia Davis

- Review of professional development sessions throughout the year.
- Discussion on areas for future growth and development.

11:45 AM - 12:30 PM | Student Wellbeing and Discipline Review

Facilitator: Mr. Noel Cunningham

- Updates on student behaviour, mental health initiatives, and wellness programs.
- Discussion of disciplinary trends and strategies moving forward.

12:30 PM - 1:00 PM | Lunch Break

- Lunch served in the staff room.

1:00 PM - 1:30 PM | Strategic Planning for the Next Academic Year

Facilitator: Principal Nadia Robinson

- Discussion of goals for the upcoming year.
- Areas of focus for academic improvement, school culture, and community involvement.
- Collaborative planning for school initiatives and events.

1:30 PM - 2:15 PM | Staff Recognition and Awards

Facilitator: Vice Principal Joan Chin

- Acknowledgment of outstanding staff contributions.
- Presentation of end-of-year awards and certificates.

2:15 PM - 2:30 PM | Closing Remarks and Prayer

Facilitator: Ms. Coleen Hayles

- Closing thoughts and reflections.
- Prayer to close the meeting.

AGENDA ACTIVITIES

Activity 1: The Student Council at your school is holding a meeting to plan the upcoming school dance. As the secretary of the student council body, write an agenda for this meeting. The agenda should include discussions on the venue, decorations, music, budget, and any other items you see as necessary.

Activity 2: As the president of the Parents'-Teachers' Association at St. James High School, you are organizing a parent-teacher meeting to discuss the academic progress of students and upcoming classroom events. The agenda should include sections for academic updates, upcoming events, a Question-and-Answer session and any other item/s you see as necessary.

Activity 3: You are a project manager organizing a project planning meeting for a team working on the launch of a new product at Shirley's Tech Company. The agenda should include discussions on project timelines, roles, resources, and potential challenges and any other items you see as necessary.

SECTION C- NARRATIVE WRITING (THE SHORT STORY)

The word limit for this section is 400-450 words.

A story is a narrative involving characters, events, and experiences throughout time. A story may be true (non-fictional), or it may be fictional (made-up). It usually has a beginning, middle, and end and serves as a means of moral instruction, entertainment, or informational delivery. Stories can be conveyed by written text, spoken words, images, or videos, and they frequently arouse feelings or cause people to stop and think.

Elements of a Short Story

a) **Characters**: The individuals or entities that are a part of the story.
b) **Setting**: The location and time frame of the story.
c) **Plot**: The order in which things happen or are done.
d) **Conflict:** An obstacle, problem or issue that moves the plot along. The conflict is either internal or external.

External Conflict:

- **Man vs. Man**: A character faces opposition from another character. This could be a protagonist versus an antagonist or any interpersonal struggle.
  Example: A hero battling a villain.
- **Man vs. Nature**: A character struggles against natural forces such as storms, animals, or other elements of nature.
  Example: A sailor trying to survive a violent storm at sea.
- **Man vs. Society**: A character is in conflict with societal norms, laws, or expectations, often fighting against oppression or injustice.
  Example: A person challenging corrupt government systems or social inequalities.
- **Man vs. Technology**: A character grapples with the impact of technological advancements or artificial intelligence that has gone wrong or become harmful.
  Example: Humans struggling to control robots or machines that have turned against them.
- **Man vs. Supernatural**: A character faces forces beyond the natural world, such as ghosts, gods, or otherworldly beings.
  Example: A person haunted by a ghost or cursed by a mythical being.

Internal Conflict:

- **Man vs. Self**: This is an internal struggle within a character, where they face conflicting desires, emotions, or thoughts. It's a battle between different aspects of their own personality or decision-making.
  Example: A person torn between doing what is morally right and what is personally beneficial.

e) **Resolution:** The point at which disputes are settled, and the narrative is concluded.

f) **Climax:** The climax is the turning point or most intense moment in a story, where the main conflict reaches its peak. It often leads to a resolution.
g) **Rising Action**: Rising action refers to the series of events that build tension and develop the conflict, leading up to the climax. It sets the stage for the story's turning point. It comes after the exposition.
h) **Falling Action:** Falling action occurs after the climax and shows the consequences of the events that took place, guiding the story toward its resolution.
i) **Exposition**: Exposition is the part of a story where the writer gives background information to the reader to make the plot easier to understand. This section sets the stage for the main plot by introducing key elements such as:
   - Setting: the time frame and location in which the narrative takes place.
   - Characters: the people who are a part of the plot and their roles, relationships, and personalities.
   - The situation or background conditions that set the story in motion
   - Conflict or Theme: The main problem, source of tension, or overall theme that will guide the story
j) **Dialogue**: Dialogue refers to the spoken exchanges between characters in a story. It helps reveal character traits, advance the plot, and convey emotions.
k) **Theme**: The theme is the central idea, message, or underlying meaning of a story. It often reflects on universal human experiences or societal issues.
l) **Suspense**: Suspense is the feeling of anticipation or uncertainty about what will happen next in a story. It keeps readers engaged and eager to know the outcome.
m) **Point-of-View**: Point-of-view (POV) refers to the perspective from which a story is told.
   - ❖ **First-person POV**: The narrator is a character in the story, using "I" or "we" to recount events (e.g., "I couldn't believe what happened next.").
   - ❖ **Third-person POV**: The narrator is outside the story, using "he," "she," or "they" to describe characters and events (e.g., "She walked to the door and opened it slowly.").
   - ❖ **Second-person POV** is when the narrator addresses the reader directly using the pronoun "you," making the reader a character in the story. This point of view creates a sense of immersion and involvement. For example:
   "You walk into the room, and immediately, you feel the tension in the air."

NB: Second-person POV is less common in storytelling but can be powerful in interactive or instructional narratives.

CSEC Story Writing Pointers

a) The word limit is 400-450 words
b) Ensure you have dialogue
c) Briefly describe at least 2 characters
d) Always describe your setting
e) Your story must have conflict and a resolution. Do not end suspenseful.

f) Always write in paragraphs
g) Use descriptive words which create vivid imagery
h) Use figures of speech and literary devices
i) Do not change or rearrange the sentences you are told to include in the story. They should appear as they are given
j) When writing based on a picture, ensure that your story line reflects the picture
k) Always use a story map to plan your story before writing it

Effective Ways to Start a Story

a) **Begin with a Strong Hook**: Immediately capture the reader's interest with an attention-grabbing statement or query.

For instance, "The day began just like any other, but by dusk, everything had changed."

b) **Start with Action**: To fully engross the reader, jump right into an action or conflict.

For instance, "She ran toward the exit as the alarm blared through the night."

c) **Introduce a Character or Situation:** You could start with something unexpected to pique readers' interest.

For Example: "Everyone in town knew Old Man Henry hadn't said anything in ten years.".

d) **Use Dialogue**: Begin with a stimulating discussion that highlights a crucial point.

For instance, "We're not supposed to be here," she said, her terrified eyes wide.

e) **Formulate a Question or Problem**: Draw the reader in with a puzzle or challenge.

For example, "How do you explain the inexplicable? I have three days to solve the puzzle.

f) **Describe the Setting**: Use vivid language or evocative language to transport readers to the scene.

For instance, "There was an abundance of fog in the air, and the lighthouse beacon could hardly be seen through it."

g) **Make a Bold Claim or Tell the Truth to Start**: Make a bold claim and entice the reader to see it through to the end.

For instance, "I was not born lucky, but some people are."

h) **Introduce a Flashback or Memory**: To create the scene for the present, begin in the past.

For instance, "I first saw the house when I was only five years old, but the memory never left me."

Outline to Write an Effective Short Story
a) Start with Exposition
b) Continue with Rising Action
c) After Rising Action is the Climax
d) This Climax is followed by Falling Action
e) End with the Resolution

Story Map

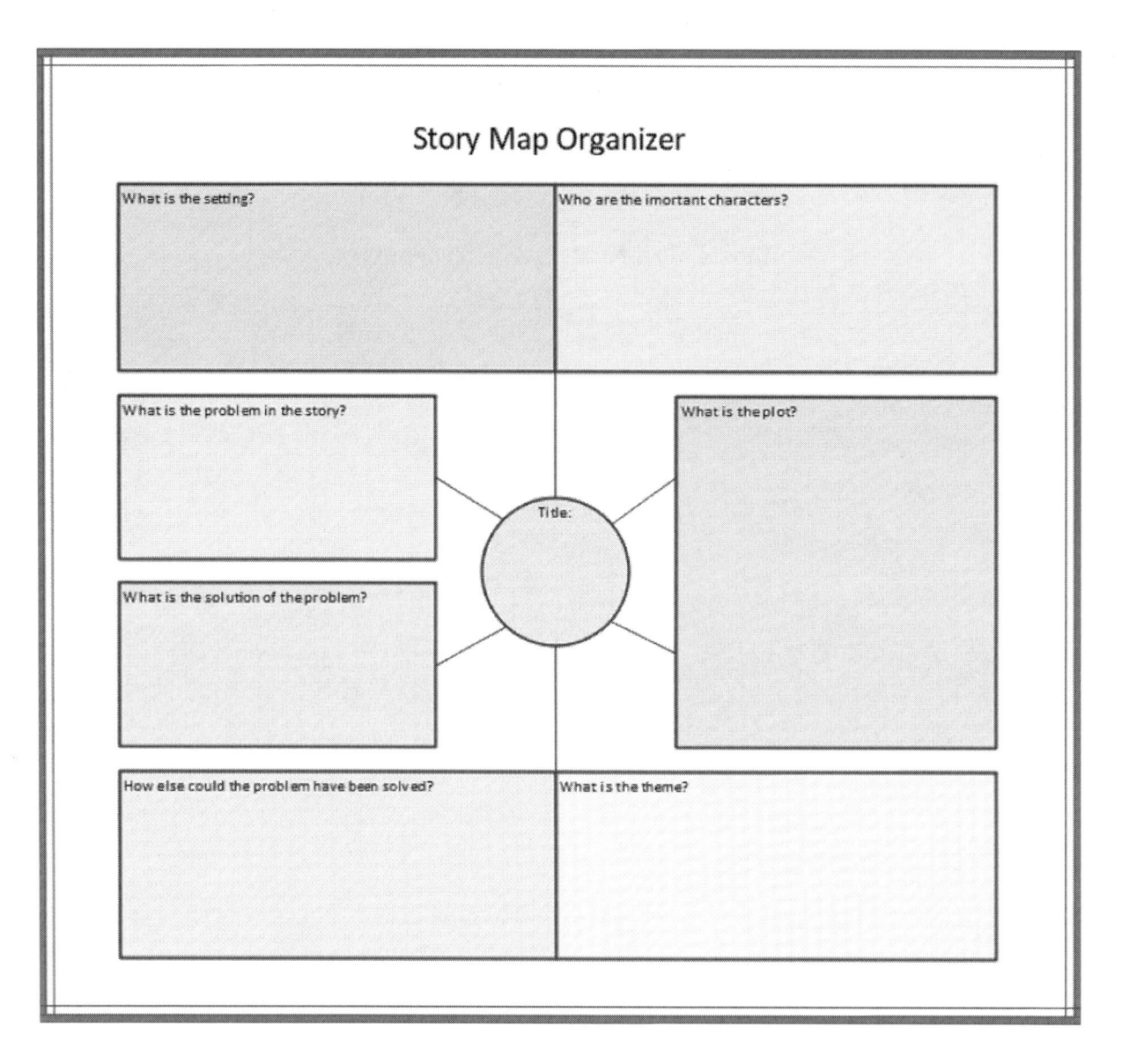

Story Map Organizer

What is the setting?	Who are the important characters?
What is the problem in the story?	What is the plot?
What is the solution of the problem?	
How else could the problem have been solved?	What is the theme?

Title:

A story map is a graphic aid that assists in outlining the main components of a narrative, such as the setting, characters, plot, conflict, and resolution. It's a helpful resource for story analysis and writing.

Below is the 2001 CSEC English "Best Story," and its Story Map.

Title: A New Beginning

As my bare feet trudged through the sludge of human and animal waste, a terrible stench permeated the air. The putrid stench of garbage, faeces, and dead animals clung even to my clothes; the stench of poverty and despair went deep inside me, wrapping around my lungs so that I could barely breathe.

I took a good long look at the pathetic shack I had called home for all of my sixteen years on this wretched earth. Broken bricks of concrete lay on the ground with no real purpose. Perhaps they had been bought with no real purpose. Perhaps they had been bought with the real intention of one day building a home; now they remain as simply bricks, the cruel symbol of a broken dream, a foundation that was never built.

The shack was wooden; the sinews and tired etchings of the wood told a story of their own. The galvanized door screeched and swung with the wind - my welcome home. Jagged edges of wood were everywhere, protruding out above the galvanized door, projecting out and above the four-square holes that were supposed to be windows. Even the light that streamed in seemed reluctant to enter. The beams of sunlight were not rays of hope; they were merely citizens under the law of physics which governed them, demanding that they illuminate the damp dirt that formed the floor of my home. The light only drew attention to the deep darkness that lay everywhere.

I closed my eyes and stifled a scream. I was barren even of tears to shed. I did not want to live here. Surely God had created me for a purpose other than to enjoy the destitution of poverty or appreciate the squalor that surrounded me. I had to believe that God was good, that He was on my side. I had no one else. My father would be returning soon. Every day I prayed that he would never return. God never seemed to hear my prayers.

Would he be returning with another man? Another ogling lusting buffoon who would try to touch me ... who would start ripping at the little cloth I wore? Would he flash the money and bring rum as payment to my father? That was the moment I made my decision. Contemplating another night of fighting and screaming and running, yet another night of knowing the weight of my father's blows; contemplating that made me decide to leave. The only thing that had held me back was the single promise I had made to my dying mother - to take care of him to make sure that my father and my brother did not starve.
I went to the corner of the shack where the angel of my life, my four-year-old brother, lay sleeping. I gently touched his shoulders. He awakened instantly. "Nathan", I said, "wake up. We're leaving." His unquestioning response indicated that he knew my meaning. We packed our few things and left. I washed him as best as I could with the river water that lay nearby. I then cleaned myself, wiping away the surface dirt and donning my only other item of clothing, a simple black dress.

Together we walked, with bare feet, along the gravel of the road that led to life. I held my brother's hand and smiled. I wondered what he was thinking. His tiny hand squeezed mine tightly. "It's okay, Edwina," he whispered quietly. "I trust you."

Story Map

Title:
- **A New Beginning**

Setting:
- **Time:** Not specified, but contemporary.
- **Place:** A poverty-stricken shack, possibly in a rural or underdeveloped area.
- **Mood/Atmosphere:** Desolate, oppressive, and grim, with a sense of urgency and hope.

Characters:
- **Main Characters:**
  - **Narrator (Edwina):** A sixteen-year-old girl living in extreme poverty, struggling with her circumstances and determined to escape.
  - **Nathan:** Edwina's four-year-old brother, who trusts and depends on her.
- **Supporting Characters:**
  - **Father:** Mentioned as abusive and neglectful, contributing to the family's hardships.
  - **Mother:** Deceased; her promise to take care of the family motivates Edwina's actions.

Plot:
- **Exposition:**
  - Edwina reflects on the squalid conditions of her home and the broken dreams symbolized by the shack and its surroundings.
- **Rising Action:**
  - Edwina contemplates the harsh realities of her life, including her father's abuse and possible threats. She decides to escape, driven by her promise to her mother and the fear of further abuse.
- **Climax:**
  - The pivotal moment comes when Edwina decides to leave with Nathan, despite the emotional and physical challenges she faces.
- **Falling Action:**
  - Edwina and Nathan prepare to leave the shack, gathering their belongings and making their way toward a better future.
- **Resolution:**
  - They set out together, hand in hand, on a path toward an uncertain but hopeful new beginning.

Conflict:
- **Type:** Person vs. Environment and Person vs. Person
- **Description:** Edwina faces both external conflict with her impoverished and abusive environment and internal conflict with her fears and responsibilities.

Theme:
- **Central Message:** The story explores themes of resilience, hope, and the search for a better life amidst hardship and despair.

Resolution/Conclusion:
- **Outcome:** Edwina and Nathan leave their bleak situation behind, embarking on a journey towards a hopeful future. The story concludes with a sense of optimism and trust in their journey, despite the challenges they've faced.

Other CXC Story Samples (Best Story)

CXC English A paper 2 question: Write a story which includes the words, "The phone rang once and stopped. It rang again. This was it now."

Beads of sweat slowly trickled down my face, the numbing feeling of guilt stealthily creeping up my spine. I sat in my western looking living room on the cowboy patterned sofa, shaking from head to toe. The dingy brown, the room had been painted, it seemed nauseating at this moment - or was it the fact that the walls of the room seemed to be closing in on me.

"I wish they would," I thought.

My mind drifted to two hours earlier that day in my classroom.
Life seemed less complex then.

"Come on Susan! There is no one here. Why can't you just kiss me once?"

My boyfriend Zack pleaded desperately with me getting more
agitated with each second that was added to his wait.
My eyes admiringly drank him in from head to toe. "What was wrong with me?"
I thought. Zack was expertly moulded in every way possible
and yet still I found it so hard to indulge in anything with him physically,
because of fear of being caught.

His caramel brown skin seemed to seep all over him.
He was tall, with full, luscious pink lips, breath-taking glassy black eyes, and curly dark hair.
The desire in his eyes drew me in,
like a fisherman reeling in his catch.

"Zack, you know physical contact at school is forbidden,
and my parents have a lot to do with my not doing anything with you. If I was caught I could not bear to face their anger and disappointment."

"I know Susan, but we've been together for three months.
I'm sure this one time wouldn't hurt, and I promise we won't get caught."

I looked up at him questioningly, praying for the Lord to restore
my sense of judgment, as I was on the verge of surrendering to him. As though sensing my wavering in thought, Zack leaned over
unto my chair and placed his nose directly on mine.
The scent of flower-scented soap softly caressed my nostrils
mixed with the baby powder smell it seemed of his youthful perfection. My heart hammered against my ribcage, almost arresting the air which tried in vain to enter my body. I leaned in towards him, and shakily pressed my lips against his.

"What are you doing?!!" A loud, accusing male voice
came crashing between Zack and me. I froze.
"Susan James and Zachary Elliott?!! This is totally unbelievable!"
the voice continued. I turned reluctantly to face
a tall, dark man, clad in a grey suit with a repulsive tie,
staring angrily at me. It was Mr Forbes, our school Principal.

"I was ....," I started to say. I was however
interrupted by Mr Forbes. "Head home now, the two of you,
and wait for me to call your parents."

The phone rang once and stopped. It rang again.
This was it now.

Like an alarm clock, all my nerves spiralled
my body into an unhealthy vibration. My mind was
jogged back to reality. I could taste the breakfast
I had eaten that morning re-entering my mouth.

"Susan!!"
"Huh!!" I replied completely out of touch with everything.
"Answer the phone!!" my mother bellowed from the kitchen.
My stomach, rotated 360°, and knotted into a
terrible bow. The phone kept ringing.
"Susan! Susan..... Susan!"

My mind seemed to be playing tricks on me.
The voice which kept calling my name seemed to be

transforming into that of a male's. A hand tenderly
rested on my shoulder and gently shook it.
"Susan, are you OK?"
I turned to look at my enquirer, and to my surprise
I was staring right into Zack's face. The school bell was ringing uncontrollably.

"Susan, I just asked you if you'd kiss me, and you totally
zoned out for about five minutes. Aren't you going to answer me?"
"Oh.... I don't think we should do that just yet.
I have a funny feeling about the outcome.

"But Susan, we've been ...." he started.
"I know, but I'm not ready," I interrupted.
"OK, I respect that" he replied, "I'll wait" quite
to my surprise. I hadn't expected this response.

We got up from our desks and walked towards the door.
"Huuuhhh!!" I was finally able to breathe.
"Thank God it was just a daydream", I thought.

CXC English A paper 2 question: Write a short story based on the picture below.

She sat at the corner with vacant eyes, discarded just like the rubbish which surrounded her. On one foot she wore a discarded men's boot which she found scavenging for food. On the other she wore a woman's shoe which seemed to be quite stylish but now had a broken heel and was tied to her feet by a string which viciously bit into her instep. In between head and toe, she wore what appeared to be various parts of clothing which had various stitches all over resembling a dirty blanket.

As she sat on the ground oblivious to the comments and remarks of those around her, she held in her hand a picture. The picture itself seemed to have been in colour but due to time it reverted back to black and white. The edges were yellow and there were many cracks in it due to constant folding and unfolding. In the picture one could barely make out the face of a young man smiling, his emotions frozen in time. The picture blurred as tears fell and grubby fingers reached out to wipe the tears away but only succeeded to remove what little was left by time. The picture was her only family, and one could see this by the way she carefully folded it and replaced it by her breast.

Getting up from her throne of rubbish she began to walk down the street much to the disgust of passers-by. She draped the little dignity she had left around her like a cloak shielding herself from their abusive remarks.

After walking for some time she halted at the edge of the town in front of a vast green paradise. A smile broke on her face, and she ran like a child into the field. A cool breeze blew, taking with it her photograph. It floated on its crisp grey wings' uncertainty, a bird now learning to fly. She gave chase and the picture seemed to be playing a game allowing her fingers to come tantalizingly close to grasp it before it sped off drifting out of her reach. She followed it into a small meadow before it drifted down landing on the ground.

While catching her breath she looked around; she had not been to this part of the field before. Flowers covered the ground in a red carpet as far as the eyes could see, and in the distance, she could see a grand old elm which stood solemnly in a corner granting shade for the younger plants. The high noon sun climbed over the old elm and burst in a golden glory. She sat on the highest throne and cast out her golden fingers over her domain. Suddenly she was filled with an unutterable joy and began to dance, oh how she danced. As she twirled around the meadow, she dislodged petals which circled her like a scarlet snowstorm. As she danced onlookers looked on in surprise at this spectacle. She danced and danced till she fell to the ground in a fit of giggles.

Looking up at the sun she lay catching her breath rejuvenating her old bones. She stared at the sun, a glittering gem in a sea of velvet. Then she saw it, a vision of beauty. The butterfly's blue and golden wing contrasted with the scarlet flowers around her. It flew lazily around her before drifting away. Getting up she began to follow its golden wings enthralling her, enticing her. She followed it back into the town and down an alley not removing her eyes from its beauty. She stumbled over crates and slipped in water still following her goal. Suddenly the butterfly rounded a corner and when she followed, it disappeared.

Sitting on a crate, realization of where she was hit her; she began to run out of the alley towards the light when several shadows slid into view. Their malicious eyes burned red wanting blood. She pleaded with them; the only response was their laughter which echoed around her in a distorted symphony. She spun around and began to run. She ran as fast as she could from the footsteps of the tormentors behind her. She ran around a corner and was trapped. It was a dead end; she whirled around and begged her tormentors for mercy, but her cry fell on deaf ears. She knelt down and began to beg for her release when a rotten fruit hit her, followed by several more. She curled herself into a ball and wished herself to a place of light and love as the rain of rotten fruit continued. Suddenly she felt a sharp pain in her neck. Someone in error had thrown a stone.

As she lay with the oil of her life slipping through her fingers, the torrent of fruit ceased. The attackers, recognizing their folly, had fled. She lay there with blood seeping through her fingers like a dam unleashed. She called out for help, but the walls threw her words back mockingly. She lay on her back, blood staining her clothes - a lamb taken to the slaughter. Then suddenly it came, a vision of beauty. She reached for the butterfly, representing her dreams, her hopes, her love but it was just out her reach. It floated on its golden wings tantalizingly close, oh so tantalizingly close. She reached with sightless eyes one last time, then her hand fell.

Practice Stories (400-450 words)

a) Write a story which includes the following words, "Sofie did not look back, she threw her tattered bag over her shoulder and walked hurriedly through the huge iron gate.

b) Write a story which includes the following words, "To this day people are still unsure about what actually happened to the Shirley family who lived just outside the village."

c) Write a story which includes the following words, "Some people never give up, they keep going on and on and on."

d) Write a story which includes the following words, "Garfield Barton was not dead; but that day he became dead to me."

e) **Use each image to write a story:**

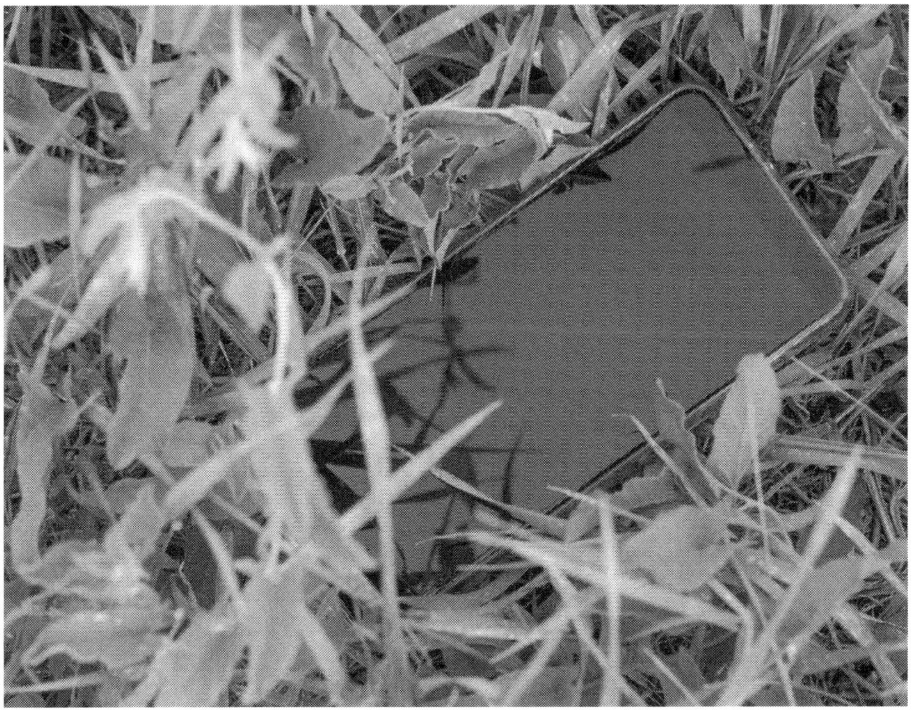

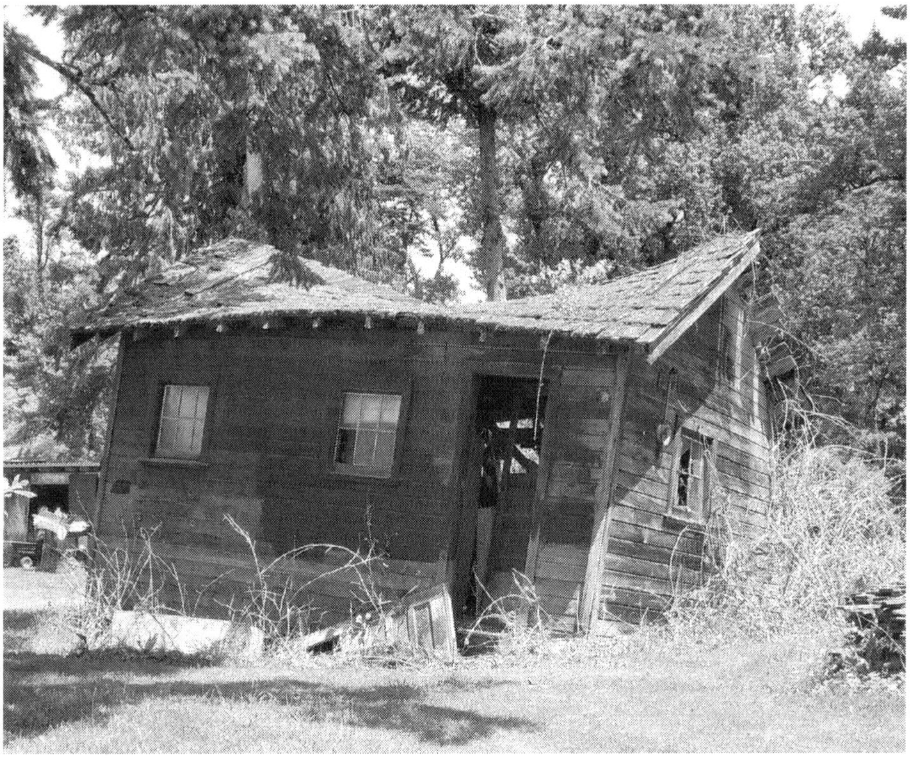

SECTION D-ESSAY WRITING (THE ARGUMENTATIVE ESSAY)

The word limit for this section is 250-300 words.

To persuade someone is to use logic, reasoning, argument, or emotional appeal to get someone to believe or do something. It involves convincing someone to act in a certain way or think a certain way by using logic or strong arguments.

An argument is a collection of justifications or supporting data used to prove or disprove a proposition, belief, or notion. It entails stating a claim and supporting it with reason, data, or examples in order to persuade others of its truthfulness. Arguments in talks or debates are meant to convince others of the soundness of a position or point of view.

The essay MUST have 5 paragraphs.

Paragraph 1- Introduction

1) Start with an attention grabber linked to the stance you plan to take. This may be (but is not limited to), the line of a song, the line of a poem, alarming statistics, two rhetorical questions, an example or a statistic. Let's say you are agreeing that Jamaica's crime problem is out of hand. You could start with Gyptian's song that says, "These are some serious times, all I see around us is just violence and crime."
2) Transition from the grabber with brief background information. You need to state a bit of information that gives the reader a background for the topic that you are about to write on. You are not usually expected to research this information. You are, however, expected to use your knowledge of the topic to do this. Limit the background information to one sentence.
3) Define the main term/s <u>if necessary</u>. For example, there is no need to define the word smoking if it is mentioned in the topic. However, if you are doing an essay on corporal punishment, it would be best to define it.
4) Next, you take your stance. Your stance is where you stand on the subject. Here, you declare whether or not you agree with the provided topic. Pick a side and write about it instead of writing about both sides of the argument.
5) Write your thesis statement. Your thesis statement is ONE sentence that states the THREE points that you will be explaining in paragraphs 2, 3 and 4 to support your stance. No explanation of the points is to be done in the thesis, just state the THREE points. An example of a thesis statement is, school uniforms should be banned in all Jamaican schools because uniforms are too hot for our climate, uniforms stifle students' self-expression, and it is too costly for parents to purchase uniforms every year. The thesis MUST be the last sentence in the introduction.

Paragraphs 2 to 4- Body Paragraphs

These paragraphs discuss the points that were stated in your thesis statement. Each point is to be discussed in a paragraph of its own. This means that, since you stated three points in your thesis, you will be required to have three supporting paragraphs (2, 3 and 4).

For each paragraph (2 to 4)

1) Mention the point in the same position it appears in the thesis.
2) Start with a topic sentence. It should be a simple sentence that ends with a full stop. Use transitional words. For example, Firstly, school uniforms should be banned in all Jamaican schools because uniforms are too hot for our climate
3) Discuss the point in a convincing way using different argumentative writing techniques.
4) End each body paragraph with a sentence that is linked to the topic sentence. For example, the discomfort caused by wearing heavy, restrictive uniforms in Jamaica's hot climate is a reason we ought to ban uniforms in our schools.

Paragraph 5- Conclusion

a) Start by restating your stance. Use a broad sentence that links back to the side of the argument you wrote on. For example, "In conclusion, we can all agree that uniforms should be banned in all Jamaican High Schools."
b) Restate your thesis using different words. This is basically a summary of paragraphs 2 to 4. Do not add anything new. For example, "Uniforms ought to be banned in all Jamaican schools as they are not comfortable in our tropical climate, they thwart students' creativity and expression of self, and they are too expensive for parents."
c) Rephrase your thesis statement (Different words, but same meaning as the thesis at the end of the introduction).
d) Give a call to action, and then close the essay.

For example, "It's time for educators and decision-makers to pay attention to what students have to say and take a daring step toward change by doing away with the requirement that Jamaican students must wear uniforms to school. I rest my case!"

Transitional Words and Phrases

Transitional words are used to show the relationship between ideas and sentences. Below are some examples:

1) As well as
2) Besides
3) Thus
4) Along with
5) In conclusion

6) Finally
7) Lastly
8) Henceforth
9) Hereafter
11. However
12. Therefore
13. Although
14. Subsequently (following immediately)
15. As such
16. As a result,
17. Firstly
18. Secondly
19. Thirdly
20. To begin with
21. Additionally
22. Hence
23. In addition
24. Moreover
25. Furthermore
26. Consequently (as a result)

Techniques in Argumentative Writing

1. **Repetition:** As the word implies, repetition is the act of emphasizing a phrase or idea through repeated use. For example, Safe to use! Safe to transport!

2. **Expert and research information**: Writing that incorporates expert information gives it more credibility. Information that offers readers of your essay experience or expertise obtained through experimentation is considered expert information. Usually, these come from people who have published in that discipline or who have an education in it. For example, according to the Prime Minister of Jamaica.......

3. **Rhetorical Questions**: This refers to the use of inquiries that do not call for a response. These are meant to manipulate readers' thoughts and make them want to agree with you by making them examine their own cognitive processes. For example, would you want your child to die?

4. **Hyperbole**: the exaggerated use of words. Here's where something is portrayed as being more severe than it actually is. For example, I am busy doing a million things at once.

5. **Statistics:** This is the application of numerical data to back up your position or assertion. For example, the survey revealed that 85% of parents of high school students are uneducated.

6. **Anecdotes**: Using a narrative or example to support a point is known as this technique. For example, this is a perfect case of the story about the boy who cried wolf.

7. **Use of Contrast**: This is where two things are highlighted to show their differences. For example, while public schools in Jamaica require students to wear uniforms to promote discipline and equality, private schools often allow casual dress, encouraging individuality and personal expression among students.

8. **Direct Personal Appeal**: In order to persuade the reader to act, one should speak to them directly. For example, I know you are tired of paying ridiculously high JPS bills.

9. **Use of Comparison**- This is where two things are highlighted to show their similarities. For example: Both public and private schools in Jamaica aim to provide quality education, by following a standardized curriculum.

10. **Use of Examples**- This is the process of clarifying abstract ideas and strengthening arguments by connecting them to relatable or real-world events through the use of practical instances or cases. For example, Jamal Brown, a student at Kingston Primary School, fainted in class on August 5, 2024, from extreme heat exhaustion while wearing his required school uniform. Given the current context, this incident emphasizes the necessity to reevaluate the uniform policy.

NB: THESE ARE NOT THE ONLY TECHNIQUES

Sample Essay

Topic: It should be mandatory that Jamaican students wear uniforms to school (Disagree)

Can you picture being exhausted before the school day even starts? Can you imagine walking to school in the blazing Jamaican sun in uniforms made of thick material due to a strict dress code? Mandatory school uniform is a controversial topic. While some contend that uniforms foster togetherness and discipline, the truth is that they have a number of negative effects, particularly given Jamaica's tropical climate. I disagree that Jamaican students should wear uniforms to school. School uniforms should not be mandatory in Jamaican schools because uniforms are too hot for Jamaica's climate, they stifle students' self-expression, and they are too costly for parents to purchase every year.

Firstly, uniforms are too hot for the country's tropical climate. Jamaica is well-known for its extreme humidity and temperatures, which frequently reach over 30°C (86°F) on a daily average, particularly during the academic year. Under these circumstances, requiring students to wear heavy, formal uniforms causes them great discomfort and impairs their ability to focus and perform well in class. A climate scientist at The University of the West Indies, named Dr. Michael Taylor, claims that "increased heat exposure can lead to lower cognitive performance in young people, especially during critical tasks such as exams." For these reasons, it is clear that the mandatory wearing of uniforms is impractical in Jamaica.

In addition, school uniforms stifle students' self-expression. According to a survey done in Jamaica by the National Centre for Youth Studies, 67% of high school students think that having more freedom to dress how they want would help them express themselves more freely and feel more at ease with who they are. Don't you believe that allowing students to dress however they like encourages creativity and helps them become more confident? By requiring uniforms, you are denying children this chance, which stunts their development and values uniformity over individuality.

Finally, uniforms are too costly for parents to purchase every year. Not including shoes, bags, and other school supplies, the average cost of one school uniform was reported by the Jamaica Observer to be between JMD $5,000 and JMD $6,000. For families with several children, the expenses mount up rapidly. Since many parents already have a difficult time making ends meet, the added cost of school uniforms may put them under needless financial burden. A flexible dress code could easily solve this issue, and all children would therefore have an equal chance to go to school without putting their family in a difficult financial situation.

In conclusion, I disagree that it should be mandatory that Jamaican students wear uniforms to school. The fact that uniforms are hot, uncomfortable, and stifle individuality, not to mention the financial burden they put on parents, all indicate that uniforms are more of a hindrance than an aid. Jamaican schools should adopt more reasonable, flexible clothing regulations that represent the demands of a modern Jamaican society as we work toward developing a more inclusive and student-centred educational system. I rest my case.

Practice Essay Questions

For each item below, write an essay either agreeing or disagreeing with each topic. (250-300 words).

a) People should be allowed to abuse illegal drugs if they so desire. Afterall, what people do with their bodies is nobody's business but theirs.

b) Corporal punishment should be reintroduced in Jamaican schools.

c) Physical Education should be mandatory for all students in Jamaican schools.

d) Schools should provide all students with free lunches every day.

e) Before graduating from high school, all students should participate in a work-experience programme.

Appendices

Figures of Speech.

- **Alliteration:** Repetition of successive consonant sounds in words close to each other in a sentence. For example: She sells seashells by the seashore.
- **Assonance:** Repetition of successive vowel sounds in words close to each other in a sentence. For example: Oh, how I love you, Lord.
- **Euphemism:** A mild, indirect or subtle way of saying something so as to lessen its harsh effects. For example: Old Mr. John passed away yesterday evening. Instead of died, passed away is used to make the harsh reality of death more subtle.
- **Hyperbole:** Deliberate exaggeration to achieve a desired effect. For example: I am so hungry, I could eat a horse.
- **Metaphor:** (i) An implied comparison between two things. For example: The thunder roared before the rain started.

  (ii) A comparison that says one thing is another. For example: The sea is a hungry dog.
- **Onomatopoeia:** A word that imitates the sounds it makes. For example: bang buzz moo sizzle
- **Oxymoron:** Opposite terms used together to paint a particular picture. For example: Love is bittersweet.
- **Paradox:** A sentence that appears senseless or self-contradictory but makes sense. For example: The child is the father of the man.
- **Personification:** Giving human qualities to nonhuman things. For example: The flowers are dancing in the wind.
- **Pun:** A dramatic play on words that sound the same but have different meanings. For example: The horse is a **stable** animal.
- **Simile:** A comparison between two things of like nature using like or as. For example: I look like my mother.

Literary Devices

- **Allusion**: an indirect reference to a person, place, thing or idea. For example:
  (i)   MOTHERLAND-Africa
  (ii)   LAND OF WOOD AND WATER-JAMAICA
  (iii) KING OF THE DANCEHALL-BEENIE MAN
  (iv)   CHEDDAR-MONEY
  (v)   WORLD BOSS- VYBZ KARTEL

- **Cliché:** An expression that has lost its originality, freshness and effectiveness due to overuse. For example: Do not burn the candles at both ends.

- **Idiom**: An expression that cannot be understood from the meanings of its separate words but must be learned and understood as a whole. The expression is not to be taken literally, but figuratively as a group. For example:
  - (i) It is raining cats and dogs outside. This means that it is raining heavily.
  - (ii) Go break a leg- This means, go and do well/great
  - (iii) A dime a dozen. – This means very common.
  - (iv) Don't beat around the bush. – This means you should just say what you really mean.
  - (v) To call it a night. – This means to go to bed.

- **Imagery**-use of words and phrases which appeal to our sense. There are 5 types of images:
  - Visual imagery (sight/seeing)
  - Auditory imagery (hearing)
  - Olfactory imagery (smell)
  - Gustatory imagery (taste)
  - Tactile imagery (touch/feeling)

  For example: He was dressed in a blue and grey plaid shirt with white jeans and black shoes. (Visual Imagery).

  For example: He reminded me of urine mixed with sweat. (Olfactory image)

- **Irony:** The expression of one's meaning by using language that normally signifies the opposite of what one is saying. The intent is simply to use the reverse of what you mean to convey what you mean. Irony may be verbal or situational.
  - (i) Verbal irony occurs when a speaker's intention is the opposite of what he or she is saying. For example, a character stepping out into a hurricane and saying, "What nice weather we're having!"
  - (ii) Situational irony occurs when the actual result of a situation is totally different from what you'd expect the result to be. For example, a pastor who preaches against infidelity (cheating) is caught cheating.

- **Rhetorical Question**: A question asked not to seek an answer but to provoke thought and bring about some sort of change in thinking or behaviour. For example:
  - Do you want to own your own home?
  - Would you want your child to die?

- **Sarcasm:** The expression of one's meaning by using language to either mock or annoy someone, or for humorous purposes. Sarcasm may use irony at times, meaning, sarcasm may involve one saying the opposite of what is meant, but sarcasm will be humorous or will be used to mock or annoy someone. Irony does not do that. For example: You deserve the punctuality award for being late daily.

NB: These are not the only figures of speech and literary devices in the English Language.

Acknowledgment of Sources

Credit is given to the Jamaica Gleaner, the Jamaica Observer, and the Caribbean Examinations Council (CXC). Brief excerpts from these sources have supported and enhanced the content within this publication.

Copyright © 2024

Reginea S. Shirley-PhD

Made in the USA
Columbia, SC
12 January 2025